Thank You for Being
A Poet's Memoir of Home

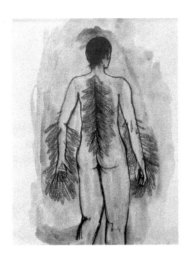

Merle Bachman

Wet Cement Press
Berkeley, California

ISBN: 979-8-9856206-0-3

Many thanks to Brooklyn-based artist Emily Church (emilychurchart.com)
for permission to use her print on the cover.

Special thanks to the following colleagues and friends:

For their encouragement and support in the creation of this book: Kristin Prevallet
and Anthony Rudolf. For patient listening and response in our far-flung writing group:
Renata Ewing, Aife Murray and Jane Perry. For deep and helpful feedback: Sari Broner,
Chris Carreher, Dale Going, Jaime Robles. For a supportive space to share my work:
Laura Lasuertmer and Women Writing for (a) Change, Bloomington. For really seeing
this book and believing in it: Barbara Roether.

And for everything else, Terry Usrey.

Wet Cement Press
Berkeley, California
www.wetcementpress.com

WCP 11-4

MAP:

The past is a blue note inside of me.
—Laura Nyro, *New York Tendaberry* (1969)

To pull yourself up by your own roots;
to eat the last meal in your old neighborhood.
—Adrienne Rich, *The Will to Change* (1971)

* * *

On her grave marker someone can scribble the words: *Never wanted to be tied down.*

House hunger sweeps through and confuses her. What does she want? If she buys a cottage, she'll never own a loft. If she owns a loft, she'll never have a garden.

And regardless, the finances and responsibilities would mean she'd never get to Wigtown, that place in Dumfries & Galloway, Scotland, facing the Irish Sea, that is filled with used bookstores and young musicians who like to play in them.

The yearning cuts both ways: house, an embedding for life.

And movement, circulating from the California coast to the Isle of Skye, circulating without impediment (as far as her money can go).

What does it mean always to be *in* but not *of* a place?

—a slender preposition that supports a glittering weight

AN OPENING

It was the summer it rained for a week straight and the girls were cooped up in a cabin at Camp Echo Lake in the Adirondacks, where it made perfect sense to focus on "M," the one who wrote poetry by flashlight under her blanket late at night. They were 13 years old, so they often said nasty things about her.

Stubbornly, she read from Palgrave's *Golden Treasury of Poetry* and reflected on her life and the size of the universe.

When you live long enough, you have stepped out of the bodies of your previous selves and can write about them as an observer. And why write only as "I"? A life comprises many selves, which can be viewed from various subject positions: so, sometimes I am "M," more often "she" or the "you" I am frequently in conversation with, in my head.

Or the "we" that, far from royal, is the culmination of our parts, and a communing with audience.

And of course you write about them, because you've always experienced life through a mesh of words. The only way to remember clearly is to *look back*: at an old notebook or a journal, to a story or a poem you wrote as a teenager, or a 20-something who is herself looking back, where you see the words "sail" "Canadian" "lake" and with these prompts reassemble what happened (e.g., that camp counselor Gary took you out on his Sunfish on Lake George, and he tried to teach you how to work the sail, to make it go "aboat" instead of about, saying it that way because he was Canadian, and that was much more interesting to you than sailing, and also he was cute, and now you had something that made the other girls give you sidelong looks of semi-respect).

Except this is not strictly true—I mean, about remembering.
Sometimes memories override the written words, or replace them.

—I met Leonard Cohen at Bodhi in New Mexico 'cos Hal and Lis got married there and at lunch the day before he asked me if I would cut his hair, back in his cabin.
But you never wrote that down—only that meeting him made you feel shy.

A friend has written her "credo," revising it over the years but not much, she is so firmly sure of her beliefs. It is one form of writing that has never attracted you. There is really only one thing you (like Oprah) "know for sure":

I have always been a poet.

And, possibly, there's a second (in credo-language):

There is something greater that holds us, that some people call "God"
(but you don't).

I could add:

If someone asks you to turn left, you will always turn right.
If everyone else is doing X, you will refuse it.

You define yourself as "different." Consider this an embrace of what might otherwise be called "not normal" (a phrase your father often used, regarding you).

This is spiting Buddhist admonishments to detach from the *kleyshas*, the feeling patterns that hold us in place, even though you know it's pointless, now, to remain aloof.

Writing is without boundaries.
One can write and write and write, as I have done, as I do, and rarely finish anything. It's like bloodletting (think of the leeches fastened to 19th century poets in need of a TB cure).

I want it all to spill, through skin, through pores, without cessation.

Call me a borderless woman, because of my life-long insistence on gestures of non-commitment to person, place, or thing (though I've had my cliché Dorothy-clutching-Toto moments, whispering *There's no place like home, there's no place like home …*).

But there *isn't* a home—in the conventional senses.
Not for me.

Still there are ways to impose structure on the odd echoes in a life, while writing about chosen, periodic displacements, while now being engaged in a process of: settling.

*

2019 was the summer of settling:
settling down, settling up; the gestures are different but find a way to relate.
And first, the un-settling:

I left my job as Professor of English at a small Catholic university in Louisville, Kentucky. My professional career had lasted 15 years (the same amount of time as my marriage, which I left after the first year of teaching). This work took me up to Medicare age, giving me the freedom to leave, to move, as I had always done (before career), but now with a notion of permanence: creating a coupled relationship once again, this time with a man who lived in Bloomington, Indiana.

So now I live in Bloomington—in his house, which sometimes feels like mine, sometimes not.

And keenly aware that, as I age, anything I write about my past is merely a frame through which the breath itself travels.

"I want to fall in an ocean of love," sings Lucinda Williams.

That's how I feel too, at given moments (given by something that feels greater than this self).

It's the ocean in which each body gets lost, eventually. *Listen O drop*, as Rumi says, *give yourself up…and take this Sea full of pearls.* How does this yearning get shared, passed around, how does it rise to the level of skin, from somewhere not so deep beneath?

After all:
Our bodies are not that deep.

An eighth of an inch in, some millimeters, is where it all happens: beats, breath.[1]

It seems, for a time, that I have wanted to sensually feel the edge where skin meets silence.

It seems—because everything (especially on this day of partial clouds, half-breeze, occasional twitch of tree-leaves) is a seeming—nothing rooted or settled or completed by its cast of material reality. It seems that the body becomes, more and more, a frame for its own living, a structure to just keep moving, through the penultimate phases. A frame that will meet its own discarding, perhaps *in Paris, on a rainy day*

---

[1] Sometimes it's deeper. They stood around the table on which you were lying, draped. This was in January 2013. It was 7 a.m. You were not aware of any of this. In the surgeon's notes, she wrote: "I made a radial incision at the 9 o'clock location…and dissected down superiorly, inferiorly, medially, and laterally 3 cm deep…"

—the poet César Vallejo's prediction of his own death, in the first line of his poem, "Black Stone on a White Stone," which really did come true,[2] but it could have been:

—*in a downpour of rain*
—*with a rainstorm*
—*in a rainstorm*

The English is in flux, because the Spanish is precise.

*

Why move to *yener velt?*[3]

I can still hear her laughing on the phone as she asked me, and picture her smile—one of "the two Chanas," the one who taught Yiddish literature at U. C. Berkeley, the one who was a touchstone, but whose student I would never be. "Why do you want to move so far away?" —Because I'd wanted to study creative writing in Montana (of all unJewish places), where I'd honeymooned with Jim, the very Presbyterian man I'd married just a year prior, and why indeed, always moving? So, I stayed and studied with

---

[2] Or so a man named Fitch once claimed over tea on the floor of a living room, where you sat with him and his woman, not because of mourning but because it was hippie days, and there was an Indian blanket on the floor. —She was your English teacher.

[3] Literally, "that world," in Yiddish, and an odd one at that. The phrase is also used to denote the hereafter.

the other Chana, the poet who taught at Mills College in Oakland.[4]

And then from California (so far from my birthplace in upstate New York) I wound up moving again, to the *yener velt* of Kentucky.

And now I'm on the other side of all that, the *sitra achra* I suddenly think—looking back. But first I look it up, to check the meaning (it's in Aramaic), and see maybe that's not such a good term to use: because it means the "other side" of the shattered vessels that Jews are meant to repair (according to the mystical Kabbalah tradition); it means the evil, the demonic, the shadow side.

Which seems to be the time we live in right now.

We—all of us—not just my divided selves.

2018, a visit to Bloomington

The mode is "natural flow" on the Mitsubishi cooling unit, so we fall asleep to sounds of wind blowing, rocking imaginary trees.

—It's the summer it rains every day for a week and then clears to the mid 90s with particulates and ozone readings through the roof.

---

[4] The late, great Chana Bloch.

—It's a summer of rising tides and heightened droughts, of dolphins beaching themselves, their round eyes never shutting.

And it's a summer of people trying to escape other people who are trying to kill them. They travel a long time by foot or stuffed into trucks and are processed at the border and have their children taken from them and their rosaries as well.

Let's call it the *migrant summer*. "Migrant": doesn't the word make you think of crawling? Of human beings, crawling, trying to get in through flimsy borders. —Online, a girl's selfie reveals a hugely swollen lip. A worm's in there, it got inside. Weak, weak. A country of 350 million people yet apparently (to the politicians in charge) so "weak," "overrun," "infested."

At the rally this morning where we stand with hundreds of others (predominately white, comfortably middle class) the mode is outrage, alternating with humor (the jokes cracked by people sweating together, trying to follow speakers who don't know how to use the mic, noticing the clever signs here and there). Your huddled masses, yearning to be free. A woman who immigrated 20 years ago from Mexico struggles to gasp the words out: "children" "cages." An eleven-year-old girl, half white, half Puerto Rican, rouses with the electric clarity of one newly born into history: "the Native Americans," "slavery," "the Japanese!" "How would YOU feel?" Speaker after speaker. We feel it: Voting is not enough. Call reps, write letters, sign petitions, send money, every, every day. One man sporting a FREEDOM tee shirt screams that it's all lies.

The late June heat makes us wobble. It takes the batteries out. After the event, buy a cookie, a paper, fix the bike. Afterwards, hundreds and hundreds still stumbling through desert to the mirage that is America. The uniformed officer: "<u>I am taking your child to get a bath.</u>" Then: "<u>You will never see your child again.</u>" Strangers in a strange land…. It's almost July 4th: fireworks and cotton candy. America and God and patriot guns. The only country in the world to have regular mass shootings. (When you first moved to the biggest city in Kentucky, you were alarmed by the sight of churches on almost every corner. You wound up joining a synagogue, another convention you'd always avoided, just to find the Jews. Self-defense!

—And Louisville natives asked: "What high school did *you* go to?"

Assumptions were made….

Can you be a stranger in your *own* land?

Now someone is saying: "My home town of Bloomington…not the capitol of Indiana but its heart." This summer of interrupted migration, lack of sanctuary, and you're dwelling on the brink of—belonging. What a privilege. Refuge among a *kind* of your kind—the "gentle angry people" (as Holly Near used to sing).

One woman in the crowd wears a *kippah*, a *yarmulke*, the bright blue of Israel.

And lo, it was the summer of 2018 before the midterms, an overheated summer of magma and forest fire and wind-stripping storms, when the word went forth from the shining city on the hill: <u>there will be camps for people who dare to run north from the people supposedly trying to kill them</u>. "Temporary" and "austere," here is where the

criminal migrants who are flooding our borders will be kept (with or without their children).
Concentrated.

In these camps.

And the summer migrates quickly, over a churning ocean, and no one can catch it or put it in a cage.

*

And eventually, you *settle*:

through the mesh of things given away, escorted by strangers out of your 8-year, Louisville flat, the place you'd lived in longest since the house you grew up in:

through the different people coming to size up, pick up, heavy pieces of furniture, their willingness to remove them, the only payment: a couple (white, tattooed) with a little boy (grandson); a couple (one Black, one white) with a mom (young lesbians); young woman creeping onto the porch and carrying off a toaster, as if she were a thief.

To settle-out: letting the grains, particulates, fall to the bottom—and there the tree outside your new window nods, though even the sound of a buzz saw that a man is using right now to cut off a few dead branches across the street creates yearning, a song of descent, the tree's sigh.

And then there is the framing up:
my partner makes a closet for all my things, and for that we need 2 x 4s and plaster board,
a hammer and a power drill.
And a gentle cloud of plaster dust, to settle.

And now that you've moved things to a new place, when you draw them out of boxes,
they are not the same:
dusty old books in Yiddish, cameras owned by deceased parents, army wind-up clock
that tells the time on other continents (but only, it warns you, if you remember to wind
it), postcards once looked at daily on the refrigerator or just bought somewhere and
never sent; little fabric cat, made into a pin; tiny wicker scottie; Barbie doll with gan-
grene on her vinyl skin.

Each thing, a fetish of the old life, the one you lived for years as a single woman (with
loneliness, laundromats, plenty of take-out—but also with a gilt edge of excitement):
sitting in a room, now, that your lover has painted for you, taking on *internal difference*,
as Emily Dickinson says (perhaps no longer *where the Meanings, are*).

But what about the stack of journals? And all the ones booted into plastic tubs, in
disarray. A life's witness to—well—a life. And the partiality of all the writing started,
abandoned, rediscovered, deemed useful…. It seems like so many breadcrumbs on the
way to the witch's house. Shouldn't a raven come and eat them? (or a fire, God forbid,
consume them, *keyn eyn a hure*? no evil eye?)

What would my mother say?

Once upon a time.... A forest of pages sprung out of my pen, typewriter, computer, in which I wander still.

1985, a few years after I moved to Oakland, California, and a few years before she passed away, I wrote:

One day last August we drove
past Burden Lake & all the
green places where she spent her
summers, growing "Why Elaine
I haven't seen you now, it's been
30 years"—old lady with the graying
face still renting boats
down by the lake. Elaine,
pleased (nothing here has changed,
wind on water, always the same,
summer to summer),
puts her arm around me—
      "This is my daughter."

On back roads in Rensselaer, in
Columbia County, through yards &
fields left to deer, doors open
and bang shut
in the wind

The Archivist Speaks

I did not know I was an *archivist*, then. I simply wrote: poems, scraps, fragments, from different locations and points of body-time. (And, writing still.) But it's the task of the archivist to order and make sense of abundant materials, both personal and cultural, literary and anecdotal, to re-assemble, structure them in a way so they are available to readers seeking connections to their own lives.

Could this be an act of "service"?

Or…is the act more existential.

As William Blake wrote:
Eternity is in love with the productions of time…[5]

A book to contain everything—that's what I want to write.

But isn't that a life? Wrapped in delicate paper, written on the inside, cells always in motion, figuring and reconfiguring until the words sink into a patch of ground.

---

[5]From William Blake's "Proverbs of Hell."

HOME, AND THE WATER BENEATH IT

In Albany, New York, where and when I grew up, the grandparents spoke with an accent, the women were large and sloped with freckled arms and sturdy orthopedic shoes, and the food smelled of onions, always. Some elder women smiled in Yiddish, because their English wasn't so good. My mother's mother knew how to sign her name but was otherwise unable to read in any of her languages (and she had grown up with some Russian, some Polish, as well as Yiddish, the *mameloshn*, the mother tongue). Meanwhile, the parents might speak to each other in a *tsebrokhene* Yiddish, a secret language so "the children won't understand" except with words like "movies" or "pizza" cropping up here and there, arousing our excitement. And there was always the *sheyne meydl*, pretty girl, and *gey shlufn*, go to bed, and a few others, some not nice, and that was it.

But my brother and I were just <u>plain American</u>, which was how my parents wanted it.

There weren't any Holocaust survivors in our midst; my grandparents had crossed the Atlantic around 1912. So the Holocaust was an education, not an inherited trauma. My family watched *Night and Fog* together when excerpts of it were shown on TV, and in silence my parents watched us watching the cartloads of stringy corpses. The next day, when my brother and I go to school, we exchange glances with other Jewish children whose parents had had the same agenda that night.

But we saw no tattoos in the realm of our family and friends. Instead, we were instructed in our difference from the Mahoneys, the Hunters, the Horans, and also fed pork and shrimp. Why not? If the grandparents had carried the Old Country with them, their children would create their own <u>country club</u> (the one already in Albany did not accept Jews), and the grandchildren would go to the best schools. For my parents, becoming hyphenated Jews was key. "Nothing but the best" and "think of number One" were my father Norman's credos, as he worked himself up from a plumber laboring for his own father to a proper businessman, a mechanical contractor. Then he relied on his "boys," young French Canadian men, to lay pipe on brutal mornings in December or July and fill up the insides of entire business complexes till everything chugged right along, and he could buy us whatever we wanted, and a new car for himself every year.

When the economy crashed in the early '70s, my brother says, Norman's business folded. Because he had always preferred to chase a dollar someone owed him rather than be generous to a friend, nobody helped him out. My parents got divorced, and he wound up leaving town. I knew he'd left, of course (I was in my freshman year at Brandeis), but I hadn't known about the context, nor did I know what had stayed a secret—and what Jewish man did this?—that mom had to go on food stamps for a while, due to dad not sending her alimony.

*

A phrase recurs in my journals:

> *I just want to keep moving.*

A list of my movements since I left my birthplace, which happened by chance as well as by choice:

Waltham, Massachusetts;
Jerusalem;
an island in Big Lake Rideau, Ontario;
Cambridge, Somerville, Brighton, and back to Cambridge, Massachusetts.

This was followed by a return to Albany for a few years, after which I left it again for Oakland, California,
then (with a husband), to Ann Arbor, Michigan for a year, returning to Oakland.

Then I moved back to Albany for a graduate program, followed by some summers in New York City, then back to Oakland (my home address for 18 years).

Then came the move to Louisville, Kentucky.

I traveled further when I could, with multiple visits to London (England) and Edinburgh (Scotland), spread over thirteen of the 20 years I lived and worked in Louisville. And now, Bloomington.

Something my Sudanese student Isaac wrote in 2002, when he was in my class at Catholic Charities Refugee and Migration Services, in Louisville—
before he moved to Seattle to work in a meat-packing plant, before he got married and had children (his American success story):

back when he was a man called a "Lost Boy," recently released from a refugee camp in Kenya to which he had walked many dangerous miles.

And was taken, sent, expedited, to the States (because this was a time when the U.S. was accepting refugees seeking asylum).

Isaac wrote: *I consider myself knowing more about the whole world … [than] many of my people and some other people … [who have] never been to another country, from since they were born until they went under the ground.*

He added:

Specially here in the United States of America, some have never been to other States apart from their own state.

When it comes to Kentucky, he was definitely right about some people having never left "their own state." Many of the American-born students I later had at my university had never been on an airplane.

And he himself had traveled so very far…Isaac, who unknowingly disturbed me once by telling me I was his "mother" in America.

Does Isaac think of Seattle as his home? I should ask him.

Maybe Isaac would ask <u>me</u> where I feel most at home.

—Except he wouldn't, because "feeling" at home is both an American concept and a privilege I have that was torn away from him, in Sudan.

Or maybe he would assume that I am now, finally, at age 60-something, irrefutably at home because I am living with a man (*married?* No—*boyfriend*, I texted him)—a new partner. 2019 would have been Terry's 46th year of marriage but for his wife's sudden death, three years earlier. "We spent a lifetime together," he said. "Now I am in a new lifetime."
And so am I.

I have never been sure what "home" means, though for some, it surely is:
from since they were born until they went under the ground.

And I am no refugee,
but I counsel myself:

stay migratory:

if they confiscate your documents, keep your mind moving.

And my grandparents were immigrants, with the force of pogroms at their backs.

1995: The warmth and disgust of family

I have returned to my hometown to enter a doctoral program in English at the State University of New York at Albany. So, I can go out for lunch with my late mother's older sister Roselee (nickname, Butchie) and my cousin Ellen (daughter of Jennie—my other maternal aunt, who had died in 1982). We are joined by Butchie's old friend, Hilda, the woman who I remember frightened me as a small child with her enormous shelf of breast (later removed by cancer, or cut in half). We're in a Central Avenue diner with a quasi-Jewish touch: greasy matted latkes, stale bread; tough pastrami (according to Butch), "tough as an old shoelace," and she should know. Bins of dirty dishes are visible from our table. Ellen bows to the old women's tough-talk about Gladys so-and-so's run-around husband—Hilda says, "she acts like her shit don't stink." Ellen murmurs something ameliorating, with her quiet, seeking-to-please voice. At the end of it, I feel like Butchie and her old crony have put a hex on me, observing my habits with a humiliating fineness: "You drink too much water and you go to the bathroom too much. Go to the doctor." (Diabetes, my family's familiar, lurking in the shadows—or so they think. But they're wrong.)

Two weeks later, Butchie's in the hospital—a heart weakness. She's frail, with large, luminous teary eyes (like Mom's were), but still tough. Wizened as Georgia O'Keefe, skin on her arms loose & blood-purpled with strange bruises.

I spend a few hours at her bedside. She's the only one in the family who can really remember anything about the culture they'd shed, and it feels so irreplaceable and I don't know what to do except keep learning Yiddish, the language that was home to them, growing up.

She remembers Yiddish sayings. She remembers *"Di Grine Kuzine"* (My Newcomer Cousin) and sings it in perfect tune. She talks about "ma," her mother Goldie, selling vegetables at the market for some extra cash, sleeping in the back of the truck. Goldie had been widowed when Sid, the eighth and youngest child, was still an infant. "We had nothing but we didn't know any better," Butchie says. "We had each other." And her everlasting bitterness over some people who looked down their nose at them: "I fought for my family," she says. She left high school early to work as a bookkeeper, to keep the younger kids fed—and Butchie was the smartest of the bunch.

What "ma" had brought "from home" (the Old Country of somewhere, Eastern Europe): feather beds, crystal cups, little-girl Butchie and two younger brothers.

"When I met someone in Albany who didn't know *Jewish,*[6] I was shocked—how could they not know Jewish?"

Before I say goodbye, Butchie asks me, in the same tone as if she were asking for a sandwich: "Do you believe in an afterlife?"

---

[6] Yiddish is not only the name of a Jewish language; it means "Jewish."

The Archivist Speaks

My best friend when I was in Israel would see me lying on the floor of my room, writing in a big red notebook and say: "Your book of secrets."

I still have that journal and many others here in Bloomington, a writing habit however sporadic that began at age 13. In boxes, these "books" have accompanied me…. For years, my life was compartmentalized in boxes.

Like the victim of some murder, dismembered, limbs tied with a sash here, feet there, head in a hatbox.

Carrying with me through every change of residence the growing written records, plus three or four boxes from childhood—the autograph book, the Barbie dolls, the letters from overnight camp, the stories written longhand, the card my best friend Laurie made me for my 7th birthday…
—and my mother's dusky sweater, her notes about the medications she was on before she died, the wavery, uncharacteristic handwriting….

Is this the kind of stuff I want to carry?
A piece of velvet glued onto the handmade card, an introduction to the color "royal blue," I knew I would keep it forever.

The boxes still hunker in closets. Some of the letters are organized: what cousin Hal wrote me from Canada and his Buddhist monasteries in Japan, what my high school English teacher wrote me from NYC, what Debbie and Margaret Anne and Janet and Gina and Danny wrote, and xeroxed copies of what I wrote them, tucked here and there.... A trail of letters through my teens and 20s, and even into my 30s.

Just a bunch of paper, stuffed in boxes, adding to my specific weight in the world. The materiality of what's past, proof-texts of my life.

It falls to me now to make sense: create boundaries. For what is the task of the archivist if not to take a welter of paper remains and make from them a structure, a space other people can enter?

Unlike a <u>real</u> archive, of course, in this one there are no order slips and no way for a reader to remove the papers (dated and undated) from a box. So I mark these offerings by the place and year in which they were written (or took place).
Paper stands in the place of bodies, I think.

I am keenly aware of bodies that no longer exist: not just of my relatives—of Aunt Butchie, who died a year after that lunch, having made it to the valiant age of 81; of cousin Ellen who died of leukemia in 2007, only 56—but also of my own, former body/ selves: at 16, 25, at 33, 41...

Body-time takes on special valence after age 60; for my mother and most of her siblings, 60-something marked the end of the road.

I think of:
the goneness of gone. The Buddhist chant, the Heart Sutra:

Gone, gone with all beings, gone to the other shore

1982, Albany

A beloved aunt grew sick and spent three months in the hospital, before I moved far away to California.

The aunt was 62. I was 25.

I would visit her, hold her dry and weightless hand, rub cream into the cracking skin. Observe various changes in light and season, outside the cordoned windows. Someone restless in the bed opposite might vanish the next day, a new someone come in, a few days later, snoring away the morphine.

What took root between us?—me and my mother's sister. It was something I was too immature to let flower. It was not pleasant to spend a lot of time at her bedside (though I allowed my mother's encouragement to lead me there). There were things I had to do, an inner tumult of excitement connected to being elsewhere, on the move, moving out of Albany in just weeks.

At that time, I was learning American Sign Language, the language of the deaf, which seems pretty ironic.

Meanwhile:
—Leaves scuffed down a blackened street at night.
—Rain's sepia smudged against a second-story window.
—Pines held curlicues of breath.

No, those were different seasons.
Aunt Jennie passed away in spring, in May actually, a day before my birthday.

Always floating, brink-trembling, half-hovering outside the physical frame. Is that my younger self? Or my aunt, pale figure under starched, scratchy sheets, her weary mouth, deep, deep eyes—?

They had finally taken my aunt off the ventilator. "Take good care of your mother," she whispered, looking straight into my eyes. "She tries so hard."

I can't even remember what prompted me to write this, years ago—about Jennie, and how I would visit her at Albany Med.

As a person, I've been a stone that skips across water.
It's a surreal bounce, never quite tasting the waves.

*

The credo:
Whatever happens, whatever exists, whatever is, there's water beneath it.

The choosing to rent, to remain provisional no matter how many years in a particular city, despite even marriage, to stay *singularly intact* (no children). The husband came and after much time and struggle, went. He provided the structure, then other structures rose to take his place and I moved on (though the new apartment was technically a 20-minute walk away from the marital home).

And I keep writing about it and not publishing, because writing is a process and there's never an adequate place to call a halt.

So, I address myself as follows:

Your mother never lived more than thirty miles from her birthplace, but you have lived East and West and now in the part known as fly-over country. And everywhere, you've lived in apartments, or with collections of individuals in rented houses where food is labeled in the refrigerator and a chore wheel hangs on the wall.

That was in your 20s, 30s.

Now you're older than Jennie was in that spring of loss and departure.

Your abiding choice: apartments, compartments, meant to be temporary zones of habitation, not "owned": so you never buy the final set of dishes, the ones for "company," you don't shell out for matching silverware, you get by with the desk picked up off the sidewalk on junk collection day—but you make sure to have sturdy shelving for books, beginning with the ones from college classes and extending from there in row after row after row. Books in the bathroom, in the kitchen, the hallway, floor-to-ceiling in some cases, because they are (apparently) where you really live: a thread of permanence: *here lives the poet-scholar* (no matter your shifting external shapes, the succession of unsatisfying day jobs).

How you missed upstate New York, when you made it to California: so even in San Francisco, with its wedding cake hills, its painted ladies (a diorama of gilt splendor, each one more lovingly restored than the next, more expensive)—even in San Francisco, a sense of lack.

At the top of a little-used path up Russian Hill, the view explodes in almost every direction, higher than the birds. Ships pushing past Alcatraz look like gray sticks, tossed by an indulgent grandmother to please her children. The red bridge, a licorice dream, peeping through cloud.

Every weekend for the first few years, you took the train from Oakland into San Francisco and wandered around with a notebook you rarely wrote in, observing the light, the houses; turning into the park, walking through its changing tree-scape, past the haunted crystal palace that was once an enormous greenhouse, with the sad sign in front of it: "This restoration will require two million...." Once you got as far as the buffalo paddock, and then out to where parkland fell away into dunes and a lick of ocean. You wrote your friends: "It's enchanted here!" You wrote your mother: "I miss you...." Yet somehow knew that small scraps of yourself were floating off into your surroundings, shreds and bits of you were mixing with the royal color of the water, the sheltering redwoods inside the Park arboretum...until after a while you were a version of yourself, diminished and hungry.

Hungry for home, the real home, where my mother's family lived, sprawled with cousins and clans across Albany, Rensselaer and Columbia counties, with pockets downstate (my father's side), claims to New York, the big city, and seasons revolving according to a childhood timetable.

Surely *home* is where the names of places sound beautiful, even if you've never been to those places and have no intention of going. Saugerties. Schaticoke Creek. Scoharie...Valatie.

Warsaw, Soroca, Bessarabia.

July 2020, Bloomington

My mother's name was Elaine.

It was a name she took for herself, to replace the one she'd grown up with: "Gitl" in Yiddish, it emerged as "Gussie" for some reason, in English, and she'd hated it. She'd also gotten surgery for a wandering eye—must've been back in the 1930s.

Wasn't she brave to do that?

And *Gitl* is a Yiddish diminutive for "good" or "goodness,"

little good one.

The Green Room

It's September now, a time of year I always feel closer to my mother's family—aunts and uncles and now some of the cousins, gone (to the other side; the other shore).

Yener velt. You tend not to have a choice about when you go there.

My mother once drifted in and out of a small green room. That's the private room in St. Peter's Hospital where her sister Roselee waited as her husband, Moe, slept, uncertain of whether or not he would ever again wake up.

Others waited in a larger green room, with out-of-date magazines and an analog clock on the wall (this was years ago). Each room was a kind of purgatory through which one would pass, and with age, the passage tended to be in a single direction.

"No backsies," I tell the dog when my partner Terry and I take her for a walk. She strains against the leash to recapture a smell, but there's only one way at this point, and it's to the park.
And then it's home again.

My mother drifted in and out of her metallic canoe.

That was another time, when she was the figure in the bed and on a ventilator, to boot.

The opening to the Islamic holy book, the Qu'ran, is also the prayer that one says at the beginning of any of the five prayer times (two more than in Judaism—was there some kind of competition?). This opening is called "The Opening," and it's eight lines long, as far as I can tell, in the transliteration. It ends: *Guide us on the straight path—the path of those whom You have blessed, not of those...who have gone astray!* (Those ones have earned God's wrath.)

But you *can* go back and forth, it seems, for a long time before you head in just one direction: can't you?

PROSPERINA: COMING INTO LANGUAGE[7]

Sometime in 2019, I read an article published in the New York Times about the Estonian island of Kihnu, where it's mostly women who live there year-round (their men at sea, all fishermen). A society of women. Oh, the home-stitched dresses, the colorfully painted houses, yellow, red, and above all, the love and education of children.... From my American perspective, it's a distant, very different kind of women's culture compared to second-wave feminism's manifestoes, marches and publishing: Kihnu's is woven, painted, tapped like an egg, and the women keep sheep for their wool and as playful companions for the children.

The article relates what happened to one ewe who would not nurse her black lamb: "This was so upsetting to me. Imagine, no mothering instinct," the woman who'd raised her reported. "So I had her killed."

Women.

Women's society.

Inseparable from children?

_____

[7] "Prosperina" is my womanly alternative to the character Prospero, father of Miranda in Shakespeare's *The Tempest*. At the play's end, he renounces magic, saying "I'll break my staff /...[and]...drown my book" (5.1.54-57).

Like many American women who came of age in the 1970s, a decision asserted itself within me, which was never really a decision or even a choice, but a knowing—to not have children.

> *So what do you call it? —The not-having-children.*
> *—maybe something like:*
> *word-mater.*

Even as a ten-year-old, drinking Wink and eating Bugles, or as a teenager with a transistor radio pressed to my ear at night in bed, so I could listen to pop music in Chicago when I was supposed to be sleeping, or craving Yardley because Twiggy wore it and drenched with weird excitement about the Beatles
—part of me was always secretly listening, assessing—storing up details.

It was only after I "got it" (my period), that I put pen to paper, writing journals (who was cute, who was nice, who was mean), then stories and, later, poems—and the words came to stay.

Have I sought to be so unconfined, in writing and in life, because in being born I was
—*haltered*? That is, cord wrapped around my neck.
This much is what I was told whenever, as a child, I asked.

Now, I see the situation more completely:

It's 1954, a small package has been delivered by/to a mother unconscious on ether, weighing "four pounds, six ounces" (yet full term). Mother rushed to surgery; placenta did not shed.
Further: first 10 days I was behind glass, in a heated crib.

> *Some days feeling sealed off.*
> *Unable to touch or be touched.*

> *You design a world in which this life articulates itself.*

1964

I tell my best friend Laurie how babies get made, when we are "down cellar" in the basement of her house (located two doors away from mine). Laurie's father is a Baptist minister. We've been observing her father's elaborately detailed model trains (truth!), which—like many things in Laurie's house—we can look at, but not touch.

We are both 10, a full decade old (as we like to say).

"Well you know the thing between a man's legs...." (She had a brother, too; of course she knew.)

And so on.

She knew, just as I'd already known (or seriously suspected) when my mother had recently informed me about "love's miracle," while standing in our small but well-appointed kitchen.

And here's something else I came to know:
"Laurie's domestic; I'm an artist." So I told myself at age 12, when I'd been having periods for almost a year, and somehow knew that "artist" meant creative and *different*.

"Domestic" on the other hand meant children. An apron tied over a big belly on which to pat hands powdered with flour, in a kitchen, with a loving man standing near you, proud of his accomplishments, one of which was your wifeliness, your willingness, your scent of sugar dough and incipient infant.

Domestic /   / Artist.

This contrast meant something to me, so internal I could barely understand its code, just: obey it.

Girl-Theory

At summer camp.
The hush at night before heading from rec hall to the bunk.
Girls standing in a knot, whispering.
One is in the center, whose face looks hurt, whose tears have wet her skin, and the rest of the girls are consoling her. "Yeah, he shouldn't've."
At the circle's periphery others ask (one in particular): "What did he do?"

The girl who reads poetry is hanging nonchalantly at the edges, trying not to look too interested.

The temperature drops on August nights, here in the mountains.
And the doors to the rec hall, for some reason, collect moths—some very large ones, as big as a man's hand.

She went with him to the flag pole, and everybody knew what that meant.
Good night kisses, right?—poetry girl reasons. Nothing more.
She's so envious of the girls who get walked to the flag pole before lights out, before Gil comes with his big lantern and tells them to get a move on, get some sleep.

And the moths seem to whisper as they cling to the tall doors.
"Finger-fucked her."

"What's that mean?"
"Nobody can get pregnant that way."
"Does it hurt?"

It's a higher order of knowledge. This is something that can happen—a boy's hand down her pants. Does she want this? It makes her sweat a little in the chill—hanging around listening over the circle's closed shoulders, nonchalant, she's just waiting for somebody to go to the bunk with, 'cos there's no moon and the fireflies are all gone.

What men are for—
that's the question.

*

What a strange thought: to *want* a baby. Children.

Swirl out the words: Mothering (s/mothering); motherly; maternal. What do you see?

I see myself as a teenager, built small, flat, bony-hard.

And never any alcohol or cigarettes, never getting high—not bold enough to pack my things and head for the big city, New York (but what kept me that way?
—*the cord around my neck.*)

Instead, my quest was always to find a quiet place to read, dream…
"yes, yes" I'd answer whenever anyone tried to engage me.
I couldn't hear them. I was *reading*.
The books had taken me with them, left a ringer in my place.

I might've been reading Yeats:

…
That girls at puberty may find
The first Adam in their thought,
Shut the door of the Pope's Chapel,
Keep those children out.
There on that scaffolding reclines
Michael Angelo.
With no more sound than the mice make
His hand moves to and fro.

Like a long-legged fly upon the stream
His mind moves upon silence.

<u>1964</u>

Disney taught us about menstruation.

Our mothers took us, fourth grade girls all, to a special evening at public school where we watched a movie with cartoon characters that must've explained something underscoring all the specialness, and we left with small boxes of thick pads, trading knowing looks.

And looking for it, looking looking until the brown stain came! —I think my mother hugged me when I showed her; she would never *slap*. —But a bra was useless, even though at some point I insisted that she buy me one.

> Here's an invisible link to the song by Gary Puckett and the Union Gap:
> "Girl...you'll be a woman...soon.
> Girl...come take my hand."

And within two years I grew to my fullest height and shed the baby fat and could barely bear to be touched or directly spoken to, because:

—*the world's more full of weeping than you can understand.*

This, of course, is from Yeats' refrain in his poem, "The Stolen Child" (and this is a trope of the fairies—they steal your baby and replace it with a changeling)—in which he cries *Come away, O human child!*

—just *human*, I see now, not girl or boy, and the fairies too, though not human, did not seem to be strictly male or female. Getting a period meant I could no longer be just "human"—or horse or bird, as I'd imagined myself from time to time—but fully gendered and capable of gendering other little humans, because that's what nature does to us. Biological imperative.

No: *societal imperative.*

1970-71, Albany

The sky's clouded; it's November, anyway, and it's full dark at 5 o'clock.

I see myself in a classroom at the Temple; it's not bad, because there are windows looking out onto a garden (not that I could see anything now, except the dark and my own reflection). A few long white tables. A piano. One of those classrooms that's ready for anything, I guess. This is where I come for Hebrew tutoring with an Israeli man whose name is (I swear) Uzi (like the gun, right?).

I am about 5' 2" tall and very slender, with long chestnut brown hair. Sixteen. Seventeen? I think I don't have a pretty face, but I am wrong.

Uzi is not a tall man, except he is, next to me. I see him now as dark—villain-dark, black handlebar mustache like Snidely Whiplash in *Rocky and Bullwinkle*, black leather jacket, dark as November. He sits noodling at the piano when I enter, bringing the tape

recorder on which he taped a lesson the preceding week. (I can't remember the preceding week—when he was probably smiling, nice, funny, putting me at ease.) Today he's not interested so much in working with me on the Hebrew lesson. He is restless, pent-up, riffing on the piano. —Is he? I can't remember anything except what he says: "I'd like to rape you sometime."
I don't think he looks at me. He says it into the piano.

"Oh," I say. "Oh, um, oh," I say. (I can't remember anything else.
He didn't touch me or prevent me from leaving.
Or was this at the very end of the lesson, so I had gathered my things and was leaving? Probably.)

"Oh."
"Oh," I say.

Albany could be like this—gray, corrosive, like old snow.

The memory of Uzi lingers. (Until writing about it, now, will convert it into a story I can forget.)

Hadn't I had a crush on him? (That made it more my fault.)
There must have been some reason to be meeting separately, I must have been his best student, the one who deserved some private lessons. (The girl I was would never have been an underperforming student.)

Note to self, now 60-something years of age: *We were at the Temple. There must have been other people in that building.* Unless maybe it was after class, maybe everyone had left except for the principal, in her office at the other end of the building...

Further note:
Nothing "happened."

That is, he did not rape me, and I never allowed myself to be alone with him again.[8]

---

[8] In my freshman year at college another fellow disclosed to me that he'd like to rape me, sometime. What does it mean to grow into a body that is considered "rapeable"? No wonder I kept my body bony for a long while...

Interlude

Albany!

Oh birchbark manifest.
Oh beaver traders, oh Iroquois who made a pact of peace in central New York.
Oh Fort William Henry and the Erie Canal, cobblestone streets washed late May by teenage girls dressed in clogs and white-winged Dutch caps, oh tulip festival near the statue of Moses striking the rock in Washington Park. The weak spring light, celebrated because it still altered the iron flavor of five months of winter.

Oh tired mother who lay down often because her back hurt, who claimed she might burst into flame (*I saw it on the news, a woman was just walking and caught fire*). It wasn't until much later I knew her monthly cycles were drying up just when mine were starting (at 11, when I loved Cinderella and books about fairies).

Oh growing growing growing, I was, into a person, a "young lady" who did not or would not fit.

Ill-fitting. A girl who fit ill.
If it were today, I might be called queer (no, I might've *called myself* queer).

*

And then there was ballet. It fit my body and its particular bent.

Summers at the Saratoga Performing Arts Center where the NYC Ballet came to perform, my parents started to take me there, and the thought occurred *I want to do that*. I began very late, at age 16, when my hips, still narrow, had already hardened against *turn-out*, the basic ballet position of the legs and feet.

—I longed for the strictness, non-breathing, the inward pull of belly-to-backbone, exaggerated lift of sternum, skinny arm raised in Russian grandeur. I didn't eat much and it never bothered me. When Cadbury milk chocolate appeared in our house, I confined myself to a single square. No breasts to speak of, so never a bra under the leotard (despite the monthly ache between my legs, and the once-upon-a-time garter belt with thick pad bunching up as I sat on it—though sometimes a dry pleasure ensued.)

By the time I was in ballet classes I used internal protection, but I was small and the blood was heavy and easily defeated me. What were periods for? I lost track. No sex till years later and barely a kiss all during high school...my best friend a girl with whom, I've come to realize, I was in love (but did not think so, then).

Sheryl & me:
laughing till we were panting.

But there was something else inside the body, its response to the *barre's* demands, the live and living music (not just Tchaikovsky but Bach, Stravinsky)—vibrating inside me, permeating me in ways I could still only respond to in words, that put myself inside the dancers I saw onstage:

> *I dream of grace*
> *that burns inside a thick body:*
> *with breathing   I am lifted*
>
> ...
>
> *A lamp,*
> *I print the air with brief*
> *line and light*
>
> *I drink air when I'm tired...*
> *I have nothing inside me*
> *but music*
> *and this fire*

Senior year of high school, my turned-in hips produced strained knees and ended ballet fantasies.

And making words even more important, a divining rod for whatever it was I called "grace."

1970-71, Ramsey Place

Listening to Laura Nyro records on the stereo in dad's home office, down in the basement (he had one at work, too, with a secretary with whom he would eventually have an affair).

Cheap brown speckled carpet, laid down on concrete. Sometimes I lay on my stomach down there, with a notebook, working on poems—I guess to get away from my brother, or my mother wanting to give me something to do. —I WAS doing something; I was thinking, dreaming, writing.

I wrote a poem that began:

The firm hush of the head—
a voice
moving like lantern light
says, Here am I
who links echo and dream
into meaning

I wrote another one that had lines like these in it:

A scarf of snow tossed down;
the earth breathes out   silence
noses upward…

[and]

A shudder distorts the air,
passes to the roots of fear
inside me: the sky sends down
its immense silence

—and then my mentor at school, Mr. Lewis, the one whose door was always open to me in a friendly, kind way so we could talk about poetry, so I could leave him typed copies of my poems to comment on—he asked me how things were at home.

They were fine, as long as nobody let it out—the pressure that was building between my father and the rest of us (especially my mother, but we were included, it was a package deal).

There was something about the long dark Albany evenings, the cold of impending winter. I still didn't drive (was not interested), and my mother had to pick me up from Temple a couple evenings a week, which I don't think she liked. She'd be smoking in the car, with the window cracked a little, to spare me (I hated it).

Was it really so dark, I mean, was it *all* really so dark, secluded, sequestered (the way we are confined at the moment I write, because of a virus)?

Albany: winter, and grit in the snow, yellowed by pee.

At least I'm a teenager, creating a secret life. I have a few friends, but no boy ever asks me to hang out. So I read all the time. (Now I remember more about the books I was reading than what surrounded me—Mary Renault, *The Persian Boy*; Daphne du Maurier....) I copy poems into my notebook; I write poems, drafting them over and over. And listen to records on the mono record player in my room, Buffy Sainte-Marie, Dylan, Simon & Garfunkle, Beatles.

And Laura Nyro, *NY Tendaberry*—a listening which made me feel in love even though I didn't have anyone, made me feel like my body was tender, special, it was berries, "a rush of rum, a brush on drum," Laura sang, "the past a blue note inside of me." It was an icy glazing that shone like mirrors, it was me seeing my own body in the mirror, it was *the Captain*, the one Laura was calling, it was New York City, all blue and silver and a scene of mystery that part of me longed for...

So I listened in my dad's basement office because he had a decent record player down there, a stereo I should say, alongside his slanted work desk and blueprints, and one comfortable chair, down where he and I talked when he'd returned from a trip to Denver (unexpectedly early? No, I think unexpectedly late, and he hadn't called my mother, and she'd been worried about him), but I was home and nobody else was and suddenly he was there and he wanted to tell me that he was going to leave her.

To leave my mother.
And I was sitting in the chair and he was kneeling, and he did the astonishing thing of starting to cry—my tough daddy-o, my father who was always either laughing or angry —crying, because—what, did he want me to forgive him?

But why? Why tell me before everyone else came home, why make me promise not to say anything, so that he could return, come in through the back door like always and "surprise" us, bring us presents (mine were orange maple-leaf earrings, made of hard plastic), so we could talk awkwardly, all of us, as if everything was OK, when he hadn't called and now mom was starting to walk off with tears in her eyes.

I already *knew*.

I was always the one to know.

Girl-Theory

A girl in my 9th grade class, very pretty, quiet, was rumored to have had a baby and given it away. Or maybe she still had it, at home. She came to school with dark circles under her eyes.

Babies, so far from my mind. My *mind*—the place where I spent most of my time, absorbing words.

I'd heard about the birth control pills our family doctor slipped to the Catholic girl who lived next door, so she could take them on her honeymoon

—only she forgot, and glowing roses petalled everywhere.

And one early morning I wrote:

> *The light roused me;*
> *I woke to find the air stinging*
> *like a gong*
> *after sound's been struck from it*
>
> *Awake yet*
> *in the landscape of sleep—*
> *a drift of details,*
> *strayed from the streets…*

the depth of common things
strengthened
in a blast of light

No early morning sun, rising like a ripe fruit
could drench me with such
silver, stiffening
on my skin, on
the bedsheets—
the moon,
centered in my window
was hurling away the houses
and the trees....

The Nucleus

The house on Ramsey Place, the four people inside it, remained.
Despite the divorce, my leaving Albany (again and again), and far beyond.

It has both haltered and guided me—at least until now, when I can write it out of my head, looking out the window of my writing room, in the Bloomington house.

The fluorescent-lit kitchen has especially hung on, relatively small but furnished with the latest in stainless steel appliances and gold-speckled white formica, which also covered the built-in table that stretched out to just accommodate the four of us: father, brother, mother, and me.

It's become a diorama lit by a TV screen and partly clouded by cigarette smoke. The china we eat on is white and (supposedly) modern. The food we eat is modern too—frozen Bird's Eye broccoli, plump roast beef, pink and faintly breathing. Strong smells, meat crackling, black coffee, "Louisiana ring cake" bought from Freihofer's for dessert, its thick patina of powdered sugar.

I am able to look around, to lift my fork, to frown or giggle. The others can't move, because this is the diorama and it all looks like displays in the New York State Museum, the ones they used to have of Indians dressed in fringed leather, carrying wampum, except—it's us. *The nuclear family*, born/e of a nuclear era (Khruschev on the TV, something called the Cuban Missile Crisis and me annoying my father by asking once too often, *Can we have a bomb shelter? Can we?*)

One learns (you learn, we learn) again and again that nuclear family is the unit: right now, even lesbians and the gay men back in California who once enjoyed queering it up want to settle down; want to sigh about "the kids" and their own devotion to them...how well the kids are doing, how brilliant they are (when you are back in Berkeley visiting, this is the current audio track), and they are so committed to social justice, they are beautiful, and their boyfriends and girlfriends are beautiful, and—every child of a baby boomer, it seems, wants to make children, make a family.

Instead of children, say: "family."
Instead of family, say: "childhood."

Only now can you see how childhood has accompanied you, a magic cloak into which you *like* to disappear.

And through this portable, velvet interior, word-spangled, you understand

    that Prospero-*Prosperina* becomes her own daughter,

    and never "drowns" but *makes*
        her book—

EMBODYING POETRY

Entering the poem as a method of leaving the room.[9]

When my knees gave out, after I'd gotten as far as pink satin toe shoes, and my parents' marriage gave out, I was left—a studious, middle-class Jewish girl, in my confinement of books and poetry.

What else could I do but go to college?

1972, Waltham, Massachusetts

My "confinement": words unfurling, blossoming.

I took my poems into a workshop taught by Adrienne Rich.
It was a year after she'd published *The Will to Change*, and a year before *Diving into the Wreck* came out (I still have both of the original copies: each cost $1.95).

---

[9] From "Shooting Script," Part II, section 8 in *The Will to Change* (Adrienne Rich, 1971, p. 61).

In the Norton Second Critical Edition of *Adrienne Rich, Poetry and Prose*, I run my finger down the list of the "Chronology" at the back of the book, to find the place where my life briefly intersected with hers:

1972-73 Hurst Visiting Professor of Creative Writing, Brandeis University.

I had never before heard of this poet.

She was friendly but serious (she was always Ms. Rich, but by my second semester of knowing her, she became "AR" in my journals). I liked her freckled face.

Her large, dark eyes burned.
A crackling seemed to surround her, in the office where we had our individual meetings, with its large, round table heaped with papers. *Ms Rich intimidates, stimulates—I can't seem to make small talk with such a person, it would be wasting her minutes—*

And a weariness surrounded her, too; she walked with a cane, all the way up the steps of the Usdan building, and filled with excitement I caught myself running up ahead of her, turning around in embarrassment to say hello. (And the above-mentioned Norton "Chronology" is punctuated by many surgeries connected to the rheumatoid arthritis she had lived with since before I was born).

I was the only freshman in a class that even had grad students in it, who were writing sonnets and aubades. And me? She let me write whatever I wished. Thank goodness!

—the exercise for November 21st for "Eng 167a," tucked into my fall 1972 journal begins with a dense three-paragraph quote from Erich Neumann, *Origins and History of Consciousness*, e.g., "Uroboric incest is a form of entry into the mother..." and then offers these choices:

Write a poem in which birth is being experienced by the infant.
Write a poem in which sexuality is experienced as death.

The words "sensuous" and "sensual" arise in my journal of that fall—but only related to my writing.

I was 18 years old, a virgin and obsessed with poetry.

Every single entry in that journal refers in some fastidious way to my thinking about images, lines, and features continual rewriting and accreting of each poem, bit by bit — and then thinking it through, analyzing it, tearing it down, balking at it, abandoning it, returning to it, *and at least I'll have something to show Ms Rich*. I mention no other academic experience, just a couple of friends and the various boys on whom I had agonizing unfulfilled crushes. (And ballet, and going to NYC to see ballet, and staying with Judy Wolf, a woman who had been my student teacher in 7th grade and was the first person I'd shown my poems to.)

11/10/72 What Ms Rich said to me a few weeks ago still holds; the inherent poetry of things; I look at things with wonder.

A week later:
I just want to say about this afternoon—I was thinking of making it a poem, but instead: the ducks bobbing on the chapel pond, turning, up and down, orange flashing; the straw flowers in the woods; the even beating of the sun; the field, all stiff with straw—I paused there a minute, imagining I was a deer with foot lifted among the scraps of snow, intent as the sun upon the soft milkweed that had managed to break from their pods—a November scene, bereft of color, or leaves, but beautiful, simple, still—

I understood I was under her influence.

Spoke to Ms Rich today—she liked the poem which made me feel good—she suggested all kinds of things to me—bookstores, anthology, readings—

References to Adrienne appear scattershot in my 1972-73 journals—a handful, really, here, there. But she's a figure in the background, a tint, a presence, as I developed the main relationship of my young life: with poetry.

And I was relentless about it.
Jan 24 (1973), 11:00 pm: I seem to be crossing some mental line—examining living for its poetic possibilities—a coldness follows—which is ironic. No, I don't <u>deserve</u> pain, only to be in the most lucid, sharp touch with whatever I have, which is plenty enough—

Jan 25, 4:55 pm: I have to beware of the "pallidity in poetry"—I can excise a lot of fat & be left with skimp & rattle. I can quite accidentally lose a lot of possibilities that way, as well.
> *—That's what bothers me about Levertov, I think—she settles for the delicate & ends up losing strength, being weak*

Jan 31, 9:30 pm: OH I hope I'm not getting smug with my images—style—(I'll cut thru to my voice, that's for sure)
> *12:30 am*
>> *and still I feel I'm restricting myself with form or expression or something—the dangers of over-writing—a certain greasiness of style, a datedness—not careful enough with language, the images may be good but are soundless—at least (so I tell myself) I'm aware—*

And yes, aware—that (from same entry as above) *writing poetry is not an asexual thing— ie neither having nothing to do with sex or self-germinating (rarely, anyway)—it is, for me, intensely sexual, not only in that it somehow releases my tensions...but also because it involves me & words, fusions perhaps, something I don't know what, on a very low (murky) level of consciousness, primal I think—*

I was writing poems about dancers—Edward Villella (who had signed my ballet shoe at Saratoga the summer before)—and about seeing a Vermeer painting for the first time, about my cousin Ellen's wedding, about frost and snow, about my mother's post-divorce anorexia, about the degradation I felt after an experience with a boy who had pronounced me "frigid."

In her office one day, Ms. Rich told me I should send a particular poem out for publication, to Ms. Magazine (I think it was). She told me, maybe in just those words, maybe right out, that a poem like that was important for other people (other women, I understood) to read.

Of course, I never did, because all I wanted was her benediction.
And I got it.

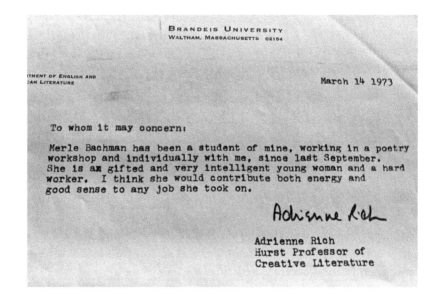

BRANDEIS UNIVERSITY
WALTHAM, MASSACHUSETTS 02154

...TMENT OF ENGLISH AND
...CAN LITERATURE

March 14 1973

To whom it may concern:

Merle Bachman has been a student of mine, working in a poetry
workshop and individually with me, since last September.
She is an gifted and very intelligent young woman and a hard
worker. I think she would contribute both energy and
good sense to any job she took on.

Adrienne Rich

Adrienne Rich
Hurst Professor of
Creative Literature

*

And oh, the boys.

One called Mike about whom I spent many hours of self-flagellating fantasy had dark hair, dark skin, blue eyes and a chiseled face. The only way I could handle his lack of interest in me physically was to try to write a poem about him and at *1:30 am Feb 5th Shit—not even a poem out of it. Such shit, shit, shit. If my heart stops pumping words I'll be dead.*

By late March, so frustrated with myself, my inability to form real friendships, to get a boy to like me (let alone love me), this entry appears: *1:05 am. Poems in a holding pattern—I feel sort of a step away, preoccupied with tests & people & as usual, myself. Questions I would ask a psych. counselor: how do I quit taking myself so seriously? I may know I need to change, but how? I'm sick of myself, I need to get away from myself—of course I always come back to me & make up, make nice, but—really. I need something to take me away from all this negative thinking. Cynical. I think of committing suicide, of course can't, so punish myself with poisons—candy, overeating...*[I probably weighed 100 pounds, dripping wet.] *I hate the fact I'm writing all this down! It seems all so irrelevant to the poems. It's an obstruction—from artistic indulgence to obstruction.*

I can remember threading in and out of depression, not just that year, but many years. But I can never remember writing "suicide" in a notebook.

Finding this startles the Archivist.
Who is this girl, this 18-year-old, inside this journal?
(Inside myself...?)

Two days later—*3/29 12:45 am: Either forcing poems or feeling alienated from them or both—seem to have lost all emotional drive, which bothers me—AR didn't dig "Rehearsal," I felt down—she said, wisely, "You'll never survive in the world of poetry if you can't take a week of [being dry]—we all have to go thru it"—months, years even, for her....*

And on the next page I write:
I'm feeling maybe I shouldn't define myself as a poet...since I can't depend on it— yet, a poet I am, the ups & downs are part of it—I go with them, not changing shape but accepting the pain of dryness with the good, & trusting, for this is myself, my <u>seeing</u> that won't change—

Meanwhile, as my second semester of workshop and private meetings with her continues:

I need to hit the library & get out Dickinson & Rossetti & ghazals-

and
AR says my poetry's much better now 'cos it's harsher, the language—

and
Even when a poem's not angry or harsh, the language must be vibrant, the rhythm urgent...

I keep worrying about importance, is this poem important? but if the language is, then no matter what it's about, it becomes important...

Once the poet Philip Levine came to read at Brandeis and visit our workshop. It was soon after publishing *They Feed They Lion*, a book of intense, imagistic working-class rage.

"They feed they lion..." Adrienne joked when he took the coffee and snacks that were on offer. And insisted he read one of my poems, which was about my cousin Ellen's marriage, which had taken place in a rented firehouse outside of Albany, and went in part like this:

Bodies thick
from making children
move easy
at weddings—
my mother like
a girl with an
aged face,
dancing with her
nephews and
brothers
    again
weightless
as wedding cake...
to melt in

his mouth
      "Your mother
bless her—"
"She's having
a fine time" the absence
following her like a halo "and
when are you getting
married—?"

And so on.
Levine didn't seem to like my poem very much.

I remember how, as they batted comments back & forth about it, they seemed to be commenting on something else, as if they were using the lines in my poem and their differing opinions of them to create a secondary line of communication, something to do with what men wanted, what women wanted.

Feminism was becoming a noise around me and a pattern, mixed with poetry, developing inside my head. I interpreted it narrowly: knowing in my gut that I didn't want to be like my mother, in a marriage that went sour and became emotionally cruel, with a man whom most women (and even some men) thought was perfectly charming but who could be careless with a nasty comment that my mother or my brother or I would remember forever.

70

A sheltered girl, no understanding of politics, just a *feeling* about what was raging around in the larger world, I had no measuring stick for Adrienne's intensity: the times I entered her office to find her staring off into space; there was, thankfully, no way all those years ago to have put her name into a search engine and found out her husband had committed suicide just two years before I sat in her workshop or that she was starting to discover her latent sexuality as a lesbian. She was a burning brand, stamping the air with ideas I took in because they were *poetry* and charged-up with a passion I aspired to—more as a writer than in my lived experience.

Back to my journal:
3/4/73...no feelings felt but immediately, the word machine turns, no feelings felt but fit in words, the hazards of being a poet

That spring, I read her poems, read <u>her</u>, with a sense of empathy and connection but also like a wondering child—

no one knows what may happen
though the books tell everything[10]

<u>*burn the texts*</u>*...*

...

---

[10] Italicized lines from various poems in the two books by Rich mentioned above. I am using them out of context for my own purposes.

To feel existence as this time, this place

...
Trying to talk to a man

...
The tragedy of sex
lies around us, a woodlot
the axes are sharpened for

(What did that mean? I felt my parents were a tragedy.
And I knew I wanted sex, with a man.
Why was it a tragedy?)

I am in danger. You are in danger.... I know it hurts to burn...
this is the oppressor's language.

When did I first hear and really learn the word "patriarchy"?

I couldn't understand until years later the depth at which her poems were enmeshed with the world, the real, actual lived world around us (circa late '60s, early '70s), and that in writing these poems she had to reinvent for herself what poetry meant, and consequently became one of the women who reinvented it for everybody.

> ...   *I am an instrument in the shape/*
> *of a woman trying to translate pulsations*
> *to images*

It took years to understand that for Adrienne, poems were not sealed, to be mailed back into the self (as I did, in notebook upon notebook) but outward to all women

> *for the relief of the body*
> *and the reconstruction of the mind.*[11]

So, feminism for me meant a tangle of ideas and feelings—that women needed a voice, that the kind of anger I had at my father could be found resonating throughout the culture, that I rejected my mother's weakness (alas, without compassion) and that even though I desperately wanted to be with a boy, a man, that was not something that should govern my life.

I took this to mean I was one of the ones who'd do it differently, who wouldn't necessarily marry or have kids. On the level of images, which is where I spent a lot of psychic time and energy, there was Gloria Steinem with aviator glasses and no children and Flo Kennedy with her slogan: *A woman without a man is like a fish without a bicycle.* They raised their fists in the air, while my mother shrank, wept (and I felt so threatened by her frailty that I couldn't understand her, and it took me years to recover my ground with her)—while my mother was "beaten" (not physically, understand) by a man: my father, victorious.

---

[11] From the poem "Planetarium" in *The Will to Change* (1971), p. 14.

It was exciting and petrifying (in that old sense of being scared *stiff*), and yet: what was this thing called *womyn* (in which the word "man" does not even exist) and *womyn-centric?*—new and terrifying knowledge, because what if —what if —I didn't really WANT to be with a man? I had to, I could not suffer being <u>that</u> different.

Because my father had once called me a "cold tomato—just like your mother."

He had to have meant the supermarket kind, more pink than red—just hard, flavorless but firm. True fruit of a non-natural realm, growing in a Price Chopper bin.

<u>And so:</u>

You're wondering if I'm lonely:
OK then, yes I'm lonely

(again, words from one of Adrienne's poems).

A UNICORN

I remember my room, how small it was, yet I filled it, exactly. (My journal, Oct. 1977)

Rooms you once lived in. The room on Oxford Street in Cambridge with a single mattress on the floor (jazzed up with some pillows), there was a balcony.... It's the room where you lost your virginity, so why can't you remember it better? (You'd slept with a woman already, perhaps that's why; your best friend, even straighter than you, a whole story, a whole friendship, in a few more years it would lurch into oblivion: but *the Archivist* must intrude to say:

—we are talking about rooms.)

After Oxford St., the yellow room in Somerville, with a floor painted dark red and walls meeting in a peak (it must have been a refurbished attic); window looking down to the roof of the house next door. The forward cabin in a ship adrift in the blizzards that shut down the whole area around Boston in '77, '78, and your roommates were elsewhere so you slept alone in that room lit by snow.

In Somerville, the women moved to and fro, speaking of: other women.

The top of my world: a rock
in the Waltham cemetery overlooking the flat
river Charles & a few factories, lazy smoke
smudging October sky.

One semester owed due to a semester missed by staying longer in Israel (my "junior year abroad"), and the short-cut from Waltham to the train back into Cambridge meant up a hill through the cemetery, where my steps went even faster (on my own, in the dark) passing the little lamb-shaped tombstones, baby ghosts.

In my 22-year-old body then.

How long I stayed a girl, and how long the girl has stayed with me (the startle of seeing my hair growing out gray, now, after more than 30 years of coloring it)

—and at last in my early 20s:
I am no longer writing only in relation to poetry.

Indeed, poems get shoved to the edges, typed up sporadically, and there is nothing to do but suffer through a mental/writing process now turned toward sex, politics, and excruciating self-labor, as in:

I am a woman giving birth to myself (from a poster popular in the '70s, which hung in the office of my bioenergetics therapist).

Cambridge: in a short blue coat, flowers embroidered on the back, speed-walking from Oxford St. to the Square,

carrying a fistful of words—& my rabbit lined fake-leather gloves—jacket collar open to the wind—feeling very much the intactness David spoke of, traveling:
'alone I get on a bus, alone I get off it.'

The Archivist Speaks

—How I admire this girl. How she exhausts me.

No nostalgia for what she was working out, trying to, for her constant self-direction (the poet-become-incessant journal-keeper):
but for her: sheer LIFE: (at the cusp of almost everything that I now see over my shoulder, in quiet valleys).

In the 1970s, the newly graduated from colleges in and around Boston went into the city to live in "group houses"—not necessarily purposeful collectives, though chore wheels and some shared meals were popular, but inexpensive transition zones. So after Cambridge came Somerville (much less chic, e.g. a grubby supermarket instead of specialty food stores) and Cedar Street house,[12] where at first you'd moved in and there was a nice couple, Alan and Mary, and Mel and maybe another roommate, and then Mel moved out and then Alan and Mary did too, and there was the young guy Aikos, the organizer who took off for the summer and left a half-eaten watermelon to rot and get maggoty in his room, but that was later, and there was Karen whose shoes were perfectly lined up under her portable closet and never seemed to go out, but that too was later, because somehow it was down to you and a new roommate named Janet to pull the house together.

The two of you: fast friends, Jews. —But you, unaware of your class privilege, and she: working-class daughter of Holocaust survivors, worked harder than anyone you'd ever known at everything she did, from stripping the wallpaper in the kitchen to reclaiming herself at a new age commune, and finally becoming a therapist.
And you are still friends.

---

[12] Into a room the size of a walk-in closet, because my "real" room was not yet ready, sitting on the floor playing Margie Adams' album, especially this, over and over, music to cry by:

When I was growing up my best friend was a unicorn.
The others smiled at me and called me crazy
But I was not upset by knowing I did not conform.
I always thought their seeing must be hazy
...

Seeing is believing in the things you see
Loving is believing in the things you love!

And so on...

© *Labyris Music Co. 1974*

Fall 1977

Cedar St. house is suddenly all about being womyn-centric: about the nation of women, the songs of women on Olivia Records, Meg Christian's *leaping lesbians*, Cris Williamson's *endless waterfall*, the women-identifying women, "*imagine my surprise*," Holly Near singing on stage with her lover Meg (did you and your one-night lover hold hands when you went to this concert? Maybe...). Janet is straight, and you are struggling with not one but two potential sexual identities, but bottom line is you need roommates, and so you wind up with two kinds of lesbians:

—the vulnerable ones: Tina with the liquid eyes and serious political inquiry, but little sense of her wealth privilege, who flees back to Evergreen College in the Northwest, and then Rosita, one of the first Chicanas at Harvard (who later flees its institutionalized and informal racism to the Unification Church, whose adherents smile, smile endlessly), and

—the powerful ones: Sandy, a big woman who calls herself a dyke and works as a call girl, a sex worker from PUMA (Prostitutes Union of Massachusetts), that's how she makes her rent. That weekend she and her lover, another buoyant large woman, stayed in bed for 24 hours, or was it 48, they just never stopped *doing* it, at least that's what she said, but all you could hear was laughter, and notice as food disappeared from the kitchen and so did cups and plates.

You leave each other notes in "an Open House Book," a decorative, blue, fake-leather bound journal with marbled (also imitation) endpapers. It's part of the Archive, now. Open it, and Tina begins:

Look at all these white pages ready for us to spill our thoughts to each other...

She then covers two pages with her distinctive black ink print, discussing her feelings about welcoming in a particular woman as a roommate, because Rachel is in a heterosexual relationship and Tina would like to live with someone who is gay. *I really respect—Janet—your feelings of not wanting to feel threatened because of your involvement with men.*

Since you are, yourself, falling in love with a woman you met at "Dance Free" (who is woman-identified but currently involved with a great, hulking man), you are more open to Tina's concerns.

The content of this shared journal, from here until Tina moves home in mid-December, toggles among these topics:

—how wonderful it is for women to live together
—how sick and tired Janet is (then, Tina, and at last, Merle) with coming home to a sink full of dirty dishes
—phone numbers for roommate leads
—political commentary, and
—feelings.
An entry from Sandy combines the latter two:

MERLE You surprised me when you asked me to leave my house key in the mailbox for Hal. Please be aware that I am very sensitive to my space being imposed on by men in this house, although you may not see things in view of that imposition (it's mainly a political one—not having to do with Hal as a person...)

In March '78, it is Sandy again who writes:

Just as I settle in here I move to another house—funny—and I'll miss this house and you all...
>   *Change is Strange.*

But change *is* the story of Cedar St. house, contained in the House Book and my own journals, in which I was "coming out" of verbal claustrophobia to write, in fall/winter of 1977 pages and pages containing thoughts like these:

>   *lesbian is a lovely word   he's so boyish & high-pitched   the sky, through glass, looks filled with snow   walked all over the Cambridge cemetery   the necessary tension of man/woman   closeness w/a man is a beautiful achievement   slept next to Barbara & had a sexual dream (I didn't tell her)   2 letters written   this is dried up on paper but alive in my mind   if I am not in love w/poetry anymore   art? intellect I think and nothing happens*

>   *Then a day like today I am too tired to think & in it steals—that mood—that tenderness toward things—I see birds circling in the sky over Roxbury   That is important!*

—and poems like:

>   *Going down the street*
>   *at night, the turning of winter*
>   *on some high axis*
>   *above me*

I stop somewhere near
O'Heany's Bar, the alley divested of
all smells, sounds

My heart, a slow life
not my own, bound
into my body   locked
in the jewel work

I look up

only on this winter
night, see

the cold flowering of the galaxy

Every day this young woman comes home from whatever temp job she's typing at and heads straight for her room to write, because words and their culture are her comfort, even as she struggles to embody herself,

The full moon, beached in clouds—meetings under the sky—
sometimes it is so meaningful just to <u>meet</u> another person,
these spring nights, when I feel
my feet firmly on the ground & the enormity of
the world around me

—spring 1978

Yet always imagining *breaking away from here. I want a home, while I'm here: & (but!)*
I want to be able to breathe,   & leave

Breathe & leave.
Typing for a living & throwing herself into so many possible identities, roles, actions:
"theatre worker," "Jewish leader," "journalist," lover of women, lover of men, men, women,
why not both, lover of having lovers, bus & subway to work, walking everywhere else,
but day trips to different beaches along the Massachusetts coast, reachable by train (still
not driving),

> *Sunday, June 11 '78*
> *running on the beach today I felt like I could've screamed to let so much go*
> *how much longer will I do a penance of sadness for all those younger years of fear &*
> *alienation, & discomfort, how THEN I couldn't be me & didn't know how—?*

A 23-year-old, then. Writing:

support from B around my bisexual crazies   baking cookies w/Gina till all hours last
December   my experiences are small but rich   a night w/B in Little Italy   FOR
COLORED GIRLS "I found God in myself & I loved her fiercely"

snowfall. reading Anais Nin on the train out to Waltham   like leading a lesbian life w/
out the sex or commitment   Talk w/Janet & Tina; high-volt, smooth flowing, connecting,
this is my home

Looking back, I see—
how fortunate I truly was, the gifts I stumbled into, the women friends especially who became mentors (before we drifted away, despite and because of our passionate entanglement), and the accidents of meeting actors, musicians, writers (*like me!* I would scribble), from whom I consciously and unconsciously drew sweetness, rapture, strength.

And the women, the men I wrote so much about, whose every gesture toward me deserved reflection and analysis, these friends and would-be/actual lovers, are—oddly —mostly ones I've lost along the way—as they went spinning out into their own lives, obscured to me, but grounded by *marriage-children-house-career*
—the dreaded: "settling."

Now (in this moment of writing) I see them as having foregone the romantic fantasies that became my own way of life, which some anxious, excited part of me constantly whispered into my deepest ear:

I just want to move, keep moving
—yet living in an imaginarium built of words.

Kind of like a great greenhouse with plants pressing enormous palms against the tinted glass, leaning toward but protected from too great a light.

*

In summer 1979, I left my fourth living arrangement in the Boston area and moved back to Albany.

My mother was still there (her cancer about nine years into the future). I think I'd lost my way (if not my nerve); it's hard to say, looking back, except to note the irony of an urge to remain unsettled that had somehow brought me into my mother's apartment. There, in a kind of re-wombing, I lived with her for *nine months*.

By October, I was at the food co-op's Halloween dance and met a boy who had a name that sounded like silver earrings: "Sterling...." (*I kid you not*...as my mother would say).

Really, he was a man: I was 25; he, a year older.
But we were boy and girl together.

So in April I moved downtown to Lancaster Street, just a few blocks from Sterling, across the Lark Street divide, where we traded keys so we could leave notes to each other stuck in our respective typewriters (his, an antique portable missing some letters). He was a musician, a drummer for a local new wave band...a real *artist*, the kind I longed to be. I started hanging out in bars, in clubs, to hear them play. On a weekend SP and MB (as we called each other) might get up at 11 (we usually didn't get back from a gig till after 3 a.m.). But then it would take him forever to pick the right record, the right music for us to start the day. Talking Heads? Patti Smith? More likely Philip Glass, something to just get us moving, stumbling into each other in the room that encompassed his books, mattress, marimba and pieces of his drum kit, all his albums and stereo equipment and a ripped armchair for reading that he'd dragged in from the street to his basement studio apartment (where light came through barred windows that faced, ground-level, into the backyard).

We'd have a whole day before us to play in, walk, visit a local museum, talk about poetry, art, music, what we'd read in the Village Voice.

It was a perfect relationship for a long while…one of those that mark a "before" and an "after." Then my restlessness kicked in, and I left for California, under three years since we'd met. The time was right (or *ripe*): as young couples around us were settling down, as bellies were expanding and organic nourishment was starting to replace late nights in bars. I remember—a girl my age standing in a doorway; I think she was involved with a man called "Tiger." (This is a diffident memory. It feels more like a dream, the kind that leaves a residue that follows you through time.) She was peaceful, smiling; they were going to move in together, in a house in the country.

It was summer again, a day in August. I was afraid to fly (too abrupt a leave-taking) so I got on Amtrak where I could see them through a dirty window, my mother and Sterling, waving goodbye; could look back at them as the train juddered away, with three days before me to make the internal adjudication: leaving again, manuscripts stuffed in a suitcase.

In Sufi circles sometimes people refer to themselves as "this one."

That is, instead of "I think/feel/perceive" they say: "This one thinks…"

A way around the *nafs* (Arabic), the *nefesh* (Hebrew), the "I," the nagging ego that drives us through this world like a truck, tire marks on the bodies of tender animals everywhere.

This one had to write, in order to assemble an ego:
(and still must write, to remain a tender animal).

And: must write about *this self* —
  the one who writes,

bearing witness to its way of being.

POSTCARDS: SUMMER, WINTER, SUMMER

It's summer 1996. My brother and I stand in front of the family house on Ramsey Place, having converged from California and Florida. We pose for pictures: arms around each other, heads tilting in. The house seems small, shabby around the edges; it's seen better days. (Our days.)

An old man comes out on the porch and talks with us. He's a retired NYC policeman, built like a fireplug. His wife would get upset if he let us in; the grandkids are all staying there, and the place is crammed and a mess.

Another time, my brother will return with his wife and daughters, and take pictures of how it looks inside, but does it really even matter?

It's summer, 2020, and even writing this in Bloomington, I see: my mother's friend, the next-door neighbor Mrs. Horan, stooping over her gladiolas, lanky and elegant in dirty gardening grub. (Her tall Virginian composure seen against the short Irish-Catholic impishness of her husband, a running joke.) She worked as a nurse, and I'd often witness her in her white dress with a stethoscope curling down from her neck.

The snowball tree, its blossoms aglow.

Dirty jokes whispered in the green cabin at the back of their yard that neighborhood kids slept in some nights in hot weather, it was called "the summer house." Dandelion wine and jugs of candied fruit she'd bring up our back porch steps; sudden trays of "hermits" ("the milk went sour, so I had to bake some.") Sharing her packs of Tareytons with my mother.

Why is this so important? The red check rubbery tablecloth on the kitchen table (one not large enough to seat her family of five children; no, this one was just for chatting with her neighbors, and it had a brass lamp on it. Maybe because I looked for love wherever I could find it, and Mrs. Horan had deep, loving eyes. She sat balancing a plate of something on her lap at my Uncle Sid's house, when she came for my mother's *shiva*, all those years ago.

She lost her husband Peter in 1994, and I still have a card from her ("The family of Peter J. Horan is grateful to God for his life, for your friendship, and for your kindness and prayers") in which she wrote

Thank you for being part of my happy memories.

*

Ramsey Place has toy trees and toy cars; my brother and I are giants who have returned to a play kingdom. In dreams, I am still inside the house, in the room with champagne paneling and a hot pink rug. I peer from the window into a snowy street, and feeling satisfied, I fall asleep—for a hundred years...

My mother had a best friend named Polly; she'd known her since childhood. Polly was short and round with long thick blonde/white hair pulled back in a ponytail, and she was warm and embracing. She was Jewish and married to an Italian man with the unlikely name of George. They lived in a modernist house built of stone, with a sunken living room and lots of hanging colored glass.

One thing that struck me, even when I was a teenager:
Polly and George did not have children.
They did have a business, in New York City.

Did they not want children? was there infertility? Or was George possibly—gay? (This would be too much of a cliché: their business had to do with "fashion.")
In any event, I was never let in on their secret, and now there is no one to ask.

When I was back in Albany in the late '70s, mom would take me out to the "country," going the "back way," out in Columbia County where Polly still lived (George had passed away from a terrible heart condition). Polly would fix a drink and she and my mother would sit and gab, and I'd hang around outside, taking pictures with a small camera, little better than a Brownie, of my shadow traced on the leafy earth.

Here is an associated trope:
falling backward into leaves, into earth.

In later days, my mother would write to me about how she'd gone out there for an afternoon, and together they'd made gnocchi and now that I am the age they were, back then —I love gnocchi, but I don't know how to make them.

And one time it was snowing and mom had to stay over and Polly made the Polish kind, sweet, with powdered sugar. I picture street lights on snow, but it was the country, there were no lights, just the shadow-white of blowing snow past elegantly white-curtained windows.

Albany could also be blue and silver.
Dutch. A book of snow. Beds in the wall at the museum, walking into rooms on an elementary school visit that long-skirted or musket-bearing denizens seemed to have just left. The silvery warming pans they used to carry fire-coals to warm these beds.

The Dutch china that was blue and white, because, I guess, it really did come from *China*: except the scenes painted on it were of windmills, not willows or river gorges.

Henry Hudson sailed up the river later named for him, so there was the river and its wooden schooners.

But Henry Hudson wasn't Dutch…he was English. *Schoon*, however, a Dutch word (I just looked it up): meaning "clean."

There was a small ring that I wore in high school with a blue and white porcelain 'stone' resting in it, on which one could see a tiny blue windmill. There was the hush of the gift shop at the Albany Institute for Art where I really, really wanted that ring, and my aunt, my father's older sister who was always bragging about being a secretary for someone in the State Legislature, bought it for me, which put my mother out (because she only worked for my father, as his bookkeeper.)

Albany:
We were winter people. (A book of snow.)

> *It froze up here on the mountain last night. 27 degrees.*
> *Winter's on its way.*
> —from letter dated September 5, 1974 (my cousin Ellen)

I had a record album of Dylan Thomas reading his story, "A Child's Christmas in Wales."

Years and years ago, years and years ago, when I was a boy, when there were wolves in Wales, and birds the color of red-flannel petticoats whisked past the harp-shaped hills…before the motor car, before the wheel, before the duchess-faced horse, when we rode the daft and happy hills bareback, it snowed and it snowed…

Yes, it snowed like this when I too was a boy, but like Peter Pan, played by a girl, always.

Mrs. Behr, my fourth-grade teacher with her flowered dresses, practical pumps, silver hair (surely she was much younger than I am, as I write this), once read to us from "The First Snowfall" by James Russell Lowell, just the first two verses (the rest are bleak):

The snow had begun in the gloaming,
And busily all the night
Had been heaping field and highway
With a silence deep and white.

Every pine and fir and hemlock
Wore ermine too dear for an earl,
And the poorest twig on the elm tree
Was ridged inch deep with pearl.

...and I remember the gesture she made when she said "ridged inch deep..." and surely every child in the class knew about the snow and its great silence.

The shovels scraped against sidewalk. The fierce glitter of giant icicles, hanging from the roof. Wind moaning, rattling windows with flung snow. The street seen from my bedroom window, slowly disappearing.

Maybe it was a womb of snow.
It's part of what gave birth to me.

*

Gregg and I stood in front of our memories, in the shape of a two-story house; white aluminum siding; porch made of brick, with the lucky horseshoe tilted the wrong way, all the luck pouring out around the number 30, 30 Ramsey Place.

We tried to lay memories down on the altar of a cracked sidewalk.

What is a house? asks the dharma teacher. *Is it the wood frame? the plaster? Is it the roof? the furniture, the dust, the floors?*

The Buddha would say: There is no *house*, only dependent parts that fall away.

I can remember some of what I remembered then, with my brother, but now as I read what I've just written, I see the past through what I *read*—not as my specific memories.

And I don't *feel* much about them.

Is that what will happen when I read this book, when it's done?

Maybe that's why I'm writing it.

<u>Excursion</u>

Of course there is a headstone in the Hebrew Farmers Cemetery that has my mother's name on it.

December, 1988, from Memorial Hospital in Albany:
*See you, my sweet—at the other end of the tunnel—*my mother had scrawled, almost impossible to decipher. "But it was a tunnel," she insisted, when the doctors nudged her back—and she was alert, and knew what day it was again, and how long she'd been drifting in her metallic canoe.

And of course you can see the stone with Jennie's name, and her husband Morty Schips, and their daughter Ellen, my cousin who died at 56.

On one of my trips to Albany to visit Sid, the last one standing of my mother's family— her baby brother, then 80—he took me to the cemetery so we could visit whoever's there (some are on the Hebrew Tailor's side, some in the Temple cemetery), and he showed me where his own plot lay.

And two years later, that's where his coffin was lowered into the ground.

The Archivist Speaks

What's the use of retelling these stories?
The characters, reshuffled and dislocated (if still living).

It's a way to narrate the larger story, of course, which is: a life. (Except, being a poet, you're not much for narration).

What's the use?

—The time the boy drowned in Kinderhook Creek, pulled limp and white from the fat inner tube where he'd gotten snarled. Your mother said: "My children will not use these tubes for floating down the creek," but she couldn't say *My children will not ride a bike, climb trees, swim in deep water"* (although she wanted to).

—The child dead at 12 after a headache and some vomiting. She was your cousin, they told Aunt Butchie that it was "24 hour polio virus" but the autopsy found in the child-sized heart, brain, tissues, no evidence of disease, nothing. You, who had worshipped her, were 7 years old.

Yes, Elaine Gail, for that was her name, except we called her "Lainie," and one memory lodged in the house at 30 Ramsey Place dates to the summer of 1961—one day in July, the day after Lainie had gone swimming, come home, got sick, died—Mom was calling you and Gregg into her bedroom [*their* bedroom, but for some reason Dad was not there], where she sat in her filmy nightgown at the edge of the bed, "*something sad to tell you,*" she was crying, and neither of you really understood about Lainie but you both began to weep, because tears were running down Mom's cheeks and it was really bad, and Gregg kept rocking on his feet and you kept walking a few steps into the hall to look in the hall mirror, to see what you looked like because you had never, ever, in all your 7 years cried so hard, in all your life.

Relatives towered over you smelling from sour perfume, from sweat, and casting their Jewish shadows like a mist (this was before Lainie, as well as after): their displacement, their tough lives, their weary knowledge of the world, but also their joy,

Zuckerman's for cookies with its floor in black and white squares, hanging on to some-one's hand, everyone's pressed against the glass case, eager, it's almost time for the New Year, *Rosh haShanah…*

> —*and who am I, the lake's daughter, the girl with her feet on veins of clay*—

July 2020, Bloomington

A month of vast heat, endless sun, and hiding from it somewhere in the big house I share with Terry.
Writing.

Difficult to sleep when I've been writing.
The thoughts curlicue together in my head, the sudden tiny shocks (while we sleep in one of our three beds, the one we call "guest bed," where we can be near a slightly open window to listen to the rain that's finally falling, all night)—

Is this what my whole life has been about?
Woodlawn Avenue, in Albany, for example.
Trying to sleep and up it comes, opening, floral, in a glass of rain:

The sorrowful face of that woman statue in the park, my mother took us walking (toddling), I looked up—

A peanut butter lunch on the back porch, my mother, white bread & peanut butter stick to the roof of my mouth
(I am three years old.
No, I am four.)

A door, a Golden Book a
phone call, a TV show, a night so hot the fish leapt from the bowl.

A door (that might have witches behind it), a Golden Book (her mouth opened and
pearls fell out, then spiders), a TV show (even the music was scary, or was it the man
who made my mother shudder, *McCarthy*, his face in black and white) and the night
so hot we all slept in the dining room, with the table pushed to one side, mattresses
on the floor, nearest a fan.

This was the year after the house on Bunker Hill was completed, out in the country,
the dream house with everything she wanted and my father had designed it but then
we had to move, to Albany, so he could develop the plumbing business with his father.

A door, a Golden Book, a clock cat with twitching pendulums and eyes tricking back
and forth, a babysitter who made us cry—

Is that it?

Over and over trying to understand—
in 1991, 92?—I typed
is it OK to keep writing & writing abt my childhood?

And now, I type an email to myself on my iPhone at 2 a.m.:
subject line *IS THIS REALLY THE SUBJECT?*

*

Another morning here, now, suddenly awake because of the rhythm of words, a stream that had opened in my head:

DA duh duh duh   DAH duh duh duh

I thought it was the question, *what <u>was</u> I then?*—because that's a line I'm obsessed with from an old poem, though it must belong to poems written by many others, and echoes
> *was* I then
> > *was* I then

But the rhythm that wakes me comes straight from a well-known translation of a Hebrew prayer:

> <u>*Author*</u> *of life and death,* <u>*Source*</u> *of salvation*
>
> *Who is <u>like</u> unto thee oh Lord*

So—I lie here thinking, early this morning—*What <u>was</u> I then?*

*

In 1979, when I moved back to Albany, it was not to Ramsey Place (sold, post-divorce) but to Mom's apartment in the "Riverhill" complex in Menands, modest, two bedrooms, one with a fold-out couch from which I took the mattress to sleep on the floor. I was 25 and knew I had to be in Albany again, but I didn't really know why; wanting to be closer to New York City, wanting to…hit reset in some way, in a place I knew was home.

Early on (well before meeting Sterling), I would take my portable record player and listen to Springsteen's "Promised Land," dancing like a maniac in my room. I'd read the ads in the Times Union, for jobs. Then I'd make coffee—a Melita pour-over—and stand in the galley kitchen, looking out the window where the early autumn light produced its clear familiar beauty.

My mother had been out of the house very early, because her job as a bookkeeper at Margolis Florist's started at 8. (I had heard the clip-clop of her pumps on the wood floors, as she dressed for work.)

When I got a job as an assistant to a legal secretary at Herzog Nichols Engstrom and Koplovitz, I took the bus downtown and worked on the top floor of a bank building at the intersection of State and South Pearl Streets. It was bustling with a flurry of business-suited people and a shop right next door that sold hot nuts out of bins and there was a "Chock Full o' Nuts" coffee sign, in neon, and…the job was something to do.

Did I give her any of my paycheck? or just expect her to feed me, as she did so long ago?

Perfume (White Witch), handkerchiefs, scarves, lipstick, pocketbooks, shoes, so many shoes: my mother.

And an adult child come home to torment the nest: (her daughter).

I had a bankbook. Remember those? It recorded something like…$500, stamped or printed in it. An enormous sum. My mother had given it to me, as a way to start over.

The name of that law firm has stuck in my head with the foundational certitude of my social security number. *Her Zog   Eng Strom.*

In Yiddish (which I had no knowledge of, at the time, except for the usual childish words)
—that means: "Listen/Speak" and "Narrow/Storm"

From my current vantage point, it was the poet in me who needed to move back, who'd misplaced herself and had to start out again from Albany.

And now a poem comes to mind, but written almost ten years later, during my mother's year of illness. It begins with a series of images:

Things Not Said

the orange roof on Howard Johnson's

the flat still surface of the dead river

the lipstick on your mouth

the way you nervously adjust your wig

the sound of someone's breathing in the house

the fields and hills, dug up from winter,
colorless

...

the houses stand
askew, yellowed
like bones some dog buried last fall

"Everything's fine here"

(one more week till your
next treatment, till you're
sick again)

By that point my father was well out of the picture. It was my Uncle Sid and my brother (though he lived in Florida) who tracked my mother's progress/diminishment. Having positioned myself in Oakland, I was too far away from the weekly events; I was not expected to come home to care for her. The fact that this gave me great relief has weighed on me for years. And so: even though she died 30 years ago, let this book serve (in part) as evidence that I have excelled at last—through obsessive remembering and memorializing—at *daughterhood*.

slate   broken branches
colors scrubbed away, wood falling
to pieces

the Greyhound pulls away
from Albany and
I am on it

leaving home was never easy
even when I was
running
—to get it right, I do it
again and again

The Archivist Speaks

An Archive is more than: shards. More than papers, letters, unfinished poems, journals, flimsy and stashed away in cardboard and plastic, meant to be carried from place to place (and then delivered, at last—not sure where). It is, of course, memory itself: images, bits of story, patterns of thinking, the way it feels to kick through grass now, July, the way you stand over a sink, scrub a pot in this large kitchen with a dishwasher—and remember the smallness of the kitchen at Ramsey Place and how it filled up with relatives on holidays, ample bodies crowded together under cigarette smoke, laughter, corded telephone ringing in the corner (near the old radiator) and the doorbell and someone's at the back door too.

I am older than most of those relatives, now, and am living again in a two-story house, for the first time since my divorce—a house that is still not "home" but feels warm, accepting, safe, sheltering Terry and me, an unplanned couple invented by the universe, no burden of years accumulated together (it's only been a year and a half). The germ of the house, its original rooms, are a hundred years old, but twenty years ago, they were surrounded and built over by new rooms and an upstairs and Terry has added a back porch and patio and there's more new than old in both our lives—living here, together.

But the Archive moved with me here to Bloomington.

Now that I've opened it up, it has become (I have become) incandescent with remembering: and it's starting to singe and I am realizing that I can un-pattern my thinking and open up to the new.

I think.

From the Archive: a True Story

On this river the current flows south but the wind blows waves and ripples to the north

—from a letter written on paper torn out of a sketchbook in careful black ink and illustrated with a crescent moon, a star, a rising sun, and a winged heart. Postmark: Santa Rosa, CA, 1978.

M had forgotten about this letter but having now re-encountered it in a box of old papers, she recognizes it for what it's become: a bit of scripture.

The man who wrote it would laugh. He was just following a river in northern California, looking back to a time he'd spent crashing at a house in Somerville, MA, where she happened to live with her roommates: K (the moon), who kept her room in fanatical order, with shoes lined up to toe the exact same line; A (the star), who'd once left a half-eaten watermelon on the floor of his room, then walked out for the summer leaving it to J (the sun) to deal with its fester and maggots; and M (the heart)...

You are still with me, as fellow travelers always are. (She remembers liking his long sandy hair and how he'd wrap an arm around her shoulders. She remembers him standing with a towel around his waist, having emerged from the shower.
And that is all.)

But she has saved this letter, and now it's delivered to her again, from the depths of a corroding cardboard box...*the current flows west and the wind tries to blow me east again. Or is it the other way around? For I feel at home in Somerville...and equally in San Francisco....* He lists multiple other cities and places on both coasts.

Conclusions (he writes):
1) either I have no home
2) or else it's all home

JEWISH, THAT OLD COUNTRY

<u>July 2004, New York City</u>

That was the summer in Spanish Harlem.
You had a sublet with a young Dutch woman who was also studying Yiddish at Columbia every day.

(Spanish: Dutch: Yiddish—
    I kid you not.)

In this city, of course, it's never fully dark, it's never fully quiet, so sleep is like that too.

An uphill walk every day, in stages: first destination, Hungarian Pastry Shop on Amsterdam; then, clutching cheese Danish and a hot tea, up and over to the particular building on campus where you finished, already sweating, by ascending several flights of stairs (preferring that to confronting your elevator phobia, an inconvenient one for living in Manhattan).

A light dress, flying.

You would not go up to the roof with Sasha and her friends to observe the fireworks on the 4th of July and drink beer. You did not want to socialize, but stayed near a fan in the bedroom (a child's room, a child's cot) and tried to memorize the Yiddish vocabulary in between firecracker bursts, a spatter of cherry bomb blasts and kids yelling.

A dress of muslin, white, flying.

Put this memory inside thick charcoal lines: you're looking back 15 years to find it, over the startling tracks of divorce, university position, publications, frequent trips to Europe (with your new-found travel gene). <u>Everything happened after that summer</u>: even the couple whose apartment you were subletting had two children and each published books (true scholars of the Yiddish world).

Yiddish, your *alte heym*, your old country.

(The dress, packed into a *valizke*, a suitcase, too small now for you to wear, if you ever did at all.)

Once, Yiddish held you too close against pudding breasts, smelled like onions and strong perfume, and even though she called you *Sheyne meydl*, pretty girl, you fidgeted, she was crushing those little bumps on the back of your shoulders, those fledgling wings.

Yiddisheh *bubbeh*, Yiddisheh *mameh*…you had to revive her with smelling salts when something upset her and she fainted dead away.

But you went to New York City for three summers, because in your 40s, in graduate school, you understood that an entire culture had existed, now lost between your grandparents' and your own generation and...you had to reclaim it. Write about it. And you found Yiddish poets who spoke to you.

For example, Rosa Nevadovska: a grand-sounding name. A sad photograph: face shadowed by more than a hat's brim, head tilted, eyes looking not at the viewer but—elsewhere.

How many times did *she* crisscross the country? —Brooklyn, Detroit, L.A.

In what city did she keep the folders of poem-drafts and finished-yet-never-published poems? Or did she take them in a suitcase with her, on her travels? (One of battered leather? alligator?). In what city and at what times did she write most fervently?

A mountain of pain presses into the lines of my poems—
And years of living and striving.
My words, illuminated by fire—
Blue veins weave among them.

This stanza is from a poem Rosa published in her 1936 book, *Azoy vi ikh bin* (*As I Am*). But really it's not, because the pain she felt pressed into each line she wrote was in Yiddish.
You wrote the insufficient English.

A Yiddish critic called her a lone woman, a lonely woman, she made a life for herself but it was not a conventional one.

Now, as you write this, you're distracted by the color of a large blue jay in the yard below, which flies into a tree that's braceleted by its own swirl of shadow.

And in an earlier year of study, 1996, your first summer of absorption into Yiddish, you jotted down:
mourning the unexpected loss:
the summer I gave up the dream of a child, saving/fixing everything—

<u>Really?</u> Why can't I remember that "loss"?
It was just the necessity of acknowledging I would never possess the seamless, age-old interweave: the Jewish home, family, domesticity; culture, tradition, a sonorous regularity.

And so, again, you tell yourself the story:

(*Alef*)

Once upon a time, the dream took the shape of a man, a Jewish one, curly hair and glasses slipping down his nose—
like Kenny that Purim night in Jerusalem, who clasped you on a narrow bed (neither of you fully undressed).

And many others in less exotic places. Sometimes wearing *tsit-tsit*, or a *kipah* crocheted by a previous girlfriend; or the romance of a *tallit katan*, discovered under a shirt. Sometimes spinning jazz and smoking pot, secular if not socialist, flanneled in L. L. Bean and willing to dispense with the pretense of anything romantic.

Cab driver. Lawyer. Part-time mime. Or: *Israeli*[13]—back when that signified a lonely outpost of ideals and not shooting bullets (real or rubber) into angry children.

Still, the point was, the cultural expectation, the foundation for a Jewish life was: a *Jewish* man:
to bless the wine on Friday nights, be a co-conspirator, a braided candle—a way to enact some tracery of Jewish ritual or communal life—that faint pattern perpetually redrawn by historical agreement.

And for years the *yearning* to find it, fill it in. To find *him*—the right man, the one who would meet you on top of the wedding cake, who would through his Jewish maleness teach you Jewish womanhood: awaken in you *the desire for descendants*.
For entering the pattern, its twists and curls, like a Polish paper-cut, made by folding the paper so both sides are scissored equally and at the same time into mirroring images.

For repetition—

---

[13] For many years, in fact, I loved not just Israelis, but the liquid sound of Hebrew speech, as they turned to each other, creating their own world in the midst of my flat, nasal, American Jewish one. All so pleasing to look at: they found grace in my eyes.

a *me and him and me and him*, writ small (written in molecular scale at first, then swelling majestically under one's skirt).

Desire for:

mirrors: patterns: repeated sequences:

—too mathematical!

Just an embrace of the totality of flesh, embodiment, which would take the place of precious language.

What need for an alphabet when two bodies link in a passion for *bringing forth*? Because people have to struggle, press into each other's clay, sticks and fluids, swarming with potential infant life. *P'ru ur'vu!* The commandment to bear fruit and multiply.

In Jewish myths, only God could create through words—speech, letters: *Va y'hi...Let there be....*

Maybe with my own clay, I've become a special kind of *ashera*, a goddess fertilized by her own words.

(Beys)

But what would Rosa say? Poet-companion?

Now that my body is of a sixty-something woman—I can dream of addressing *her*, a poet in a simple felt coat and plush hat.

I put her into a night of snow in Brooklyn, Pitkin Street, 1954:

Can you tell me of your Bialystok roots? Look, I know the snow is falling faster now, and your dark blue hat gleams half-silver—but when did you begin to write? Did the poems overtake you, unexpected, at moments between washing clothes and grinding meat? Did you always think in Yiddish, not in Russian or Polish? Why did you never once return to Europe, even after the war? Why do your poems describe both empty shorelines and skyscrapers?

Rosa, holding a paper bag of groceries close to her chest, looks at me with mild pale eyes. She has dropped a mitten. A gust of wind has blown snow onto the narrow margin of stockinged legs between skirt and boots. Suddenly she appears quite young. Her thick body collects darkness in a world that values easy, blowing silver. At home, a cat is sleeping by the radiator; a pot of peeled potatoes bathes in icy water. She closes her eyes.

She married twice but also divorced.

I imagine she's had lovers.

She did have a child: *Leah-le*, little Leah—who died at the age of two during a winter of intense snow and cold in Moscow, where somehow Rosa had wound up during WW I.

In the dream there is no one else on the street but the two of us, the mercury's falling, her poems fill drawers in her small apartment, aromatic and silent.

Only one book published during her lifetime.

<u>November 1989</u>

Landscape from New York to Philadelphia seen from Amtrak windows after hospital
visit with my mother.

—abandoned factories. miles of decaying brick under thick battened sky.
& still-inhabited tenements—ropes and coils of buildings, scraps of curtains
busted up cars   trash dumped the length of entire highways.   squat blocks of blasted
windows
decorated with *fuck you* graffiti
Trenton Makes the World Takes
toilet seat factory woolen mill—and what she

leaves behind for
me: a sweater knitted from cigarette smoke
        shoes   each one widened by the pressure
over time   of her flat-foot walk

Whisper this: *blind hem-stitch.*
        There is nothing that does not
        fade to black

—and who am I, the lake's daughter... My young mother,
reading (though it looks like me).

Sisters: Elaine, Jennie, Butchie

Elaine and Norman—an early photo.

My mother smokes and muses
(possibly before I came along).

My brother and I in the back yard at Ramsey Place, on a hot summer day.

Taking a break from Cedar St. house:
me and Janet at the beach (1978).

yummy
fantasy
#3:

Yes! Lets pick apples next fall!

Kim

visit
after 4th of January

Good morning Merle —
I may not see you for but a
brief moment tonight so I
wish you a good bettering
(REALLY!) and two good days

A page from the roommate House Book.

An invitation from Jerusalem.

Blossoming in Israel (1975).

Artist's House — I had
Hummus (tasted a little
like Halavah — sesame)
This a artist school —
an exhibit of children's
drawing in entrance hall.
We had lunch in the
back yard — a bird is
singing — today is a
little cooler — much better —
a lovely breeze and sunny.
~~Dinner at the~~
Meet family by name of
Smolin M.D at dinner (Alpin)
arrived today — Son is being Bar Mitzvah Sat.
Chau Theatre —
Inbal Dance Co. Tonite
noon — instrument
78 strings — 3 legs — very

A page from Elaine's travel diary: her time visiting
me in Jerusalem.

The young poet.

FORGETTING JERUSALEM

An image of a building in Jerusalem, a house of some sort, drifts up. I have tried to make a poem out of it; untrue, unsure.

But it's a white cupola, a paleness, round yet fragmented, against a paler sky. An image that could rest against the page of a book (and perhaps does, and that's where I take it from.)

Visualizing this image makes me feel a small dazzle of warmth. Jerusalem: what was that "home" once like?

There were live fish in a tank in the supermarket.
Curiosity, then a sharp scent of citron.

Maybe I should go?   Back there?

Perhaps to witness *in-situ* the organs of destruction, the choking voluptuous waste:
Architecture as fundamentalism.
Four-star hotels as *halakha*, Jewish law.

What is it like to live there—now? (As a Jew, as supporter of the near-defunct Israeli peace movement, as a woman well past the climacteric?)

To create a small life, sheltered under a fig tree—possible?—avoiding the occasional terror of—stabbings? (It used to be buses, bursting apart, or the open market on an average day. Now there's a wall and it's Palestinians who are regularly terrorized, on their side of it.)

Photo

In a volume of historic photographs of early (*nascent*) Israel—I can call it to mind right now, and it becomes a mini-video from the 1950s, post Holocaust:

a woman (refugee) just arriving on *terra firma* (off the ship), *terra sancta*, surrounded by fellow pale-faces, European skins squirming under vertical light:

baby in her plush arms, its face pushed into her full breast, and her face lifted to the sun, eyes squeezed shut, mouth smiling to itself—ecstatic.

The suckling sucks the mother's teat, quenches its age-old thirst with the cool creamy womanly sap. The infant nurses. The mother, relieved—her breasts were swollen, painful—relieved, having reached a place out of danger with her baby, emblem of the next generation, in her arms.

Israel: where family becomes a politics, a duty.

But Jerusalem—once upon a time, the holy city was central to my *geography of long-ing:*[14] the strange yearning I felt before arriving there, the way it occupied my mind (yes, invaded and occupied it) for years after my return to the States, and the way in which I longed for it even when I lived there.

In 1974-75, I kept a faithful journal while living in Jerusalem on my "junior year abroad." It's one of the largest—5 subject, 250 sheets, college ruled, faded red cover marked with a postcard of Adam from the Sistine Chapel (his sensuous shoulders, chest). The journal itself is heavily redolent with the emotions (hormones) of my 20-year-old self...all so internalized. As if the only Jerusalem that really existed was inside my head. No people (well, except for handsome Israeli soldiers); no clamor; no violence. Just light on stone... and poems, those I copied-in and those I wrote myself.

What kind of place is this? I began, that July: *the night*
a cut half of pomegranate, so full
the stars slide to earth
where the air is dark and ripe
with the possibility—

something moving through the streets at night
breeds dogs with three legs

---

[14] From "Writing Space" in *Poetics of Dislocation* (2009) by the late Indian American poet, literary critic, and memoirist, Meena Alexander (p. 177).

and shriveled cats   the muezzin's
whisper enters my window

...and so on.

Later in the summer I wrote:

We drive past the hill that is a breast
a hip
the tender place inside a thigh
spread open in the sun
disappearing again into the sandy
soil good only for goats' teeth
Nothing moves
but strains together, full
towards the sky—longing
longing—
the bite of goats
the kicking feet of shepherds
        of soldiers

...and in late fall,

submit, submit you say.
Know you are nothing.

I walk in Jerusalem
shoving my way through people and all I see
are stones,
stones and beggars

Actually, I wrote a lot. Almost every page, a poem, or a detailed description of something never before witnessed, never before felt: and even then had the insight to jot

So many odds—ends—impressions of my body—Jerusalem—sex

and

what does it mean to
have my mother's eyes
my mother's mouth?

Yes, my mother was there. She came to visit in October 1974.
But let me backtrack a bit:

In 1974, especially to a naive American traveler, Jerusalem was a very far-away place. To live there meant turgid phone service, if you wanted to place an international call; televisions had only one channel (government-run); theaters showed "foreign" (American) films six months to a year after they came out.

—Not everyone spoke English.

—There was no McDonald's on Ben Yehuda Mall (there was no Mall off Ben Yehuda street)—although there was a Pizza Barn and a restaurant beloved by many American students called "Chocolate Soup."

There were still buses you could take from the city center to towns on the West Bank ("Arab buses," filled with jangle, noise, nasal music).

There were still parts of West Jerusalem's edge, looking toward the Judaean hills, that were undeveloped fields, open prospects: shepherd boys tended goats in fields near *Mishkenot Sha'ananim* (Hebrew for "tranquil dwellings"), where you could poke around in a sparsely populated area near thin groves of olive trees; before the '67 war, it had been a no man's land, tempting for snipers.

—And the views of those hills in Judaea, a wilderness barren and aglow with heat, heightened a sense of mystery and desertion.

Downtown Jerusalem was depressed, grimy, yet offered little curving streets off the main ones, Jaffa and Ben Yehuda, leading to odd, compelling places, like the former bomb shelter in which I took yoga classes taught by Catherine, a young French woman (who, I learned later, was herself studying Kabbalah with a Jerusalem mystic called Madame Colette).

In 1974, I was studying at the "Hiatt Institute" in Jerusalem, a Brandeis-associated program with a total of about 50 students who were housed with various landladies throughout the neighborhood: Talbiyah, one of the formerly Arab,[15] west Jerusalem neighborhoods, and the Institute was housed in one of the beautiful, formerly Arab houses, two stories with high ceilings and tile floors within and faced with glowing Jerusalem stone—and my landlady lived in the flat upstairs, and so did my roommate and I.

Israel, we learned, was called *ha'aretz*, meaning "the land," because it was THE land, because it was the Jewish nation, but it really was our student playground: ample room to fall in love, grow long snaky hair, smoke hashish (if you wanted) with scruffy young Israelis. "Junior year abroad": finishing school of young American Jews. The Arabic word *talbiyah*, on the other hand, according to the online Hajj & Umrah Planner, is a "devotional prayer" chanted by Muslims making their pilgrimage to Mecca…and though I knew nothing about such things, then, I'd bought the requisite *keffiyeh* and a Bedouin dress in the Old City, skipped my seminar on the History of the State, and gone wandering through the narrow streets and stony fields.

Yes, Palestinians were "Arabs" and Arabs were serving me at the dairy restaurant, scrubbing the stairs at Hiatt, hammering the bones of some new apartment building—always present yet always at the periphery. To me, what was most electric about *ha'aretz* was its other-culture aura: the devastating heat; closure of shops after lunch until late in the day, during summer; foods like the then-exotic falafel and baba ganoush; sitting on floor pillows at a professor's house, drinking mint and cinnamon tea out of tiny cups, around a hammered copper table. Was this *Jewish*—? It was not the kind of Ashkenazi (Eastern European) Jewish culture I'd grown up with. And of course, seen in retrospect,

---

[15] That is, Palestinian—though that name and identity were barely recognized in those days.

it smacked of *Orientalism*—except for the fact that my professor's wife, Lita, a beautiful sparrow-like woman with long black hair, was *Sephardic*: she came from a Jewish community on Dutch Caribbean Curaçao. She kept bottles with sticks of vanilla in them, to dry, along the stone windowsills of her kitchen.

—But the Jerusalem I dreamed of, even as I lived there, had no real people in it, because in a way, that had been my training: to focus on little but ruins and traces of the ancient Jewish past. I remember Lita because she was Jewish-exotic (and because she kept living and changing and became a writer/photographer). But I did not pay much attention to the *Mizrachim*, who spoke Hebrew with the accent of their first language, Arabic, who worked in kitchens and clean-up crews, dragged shrieking children by their chubby arms along the street, and lived in places like Katamon, a neighborhood where I volunteered to tutor English and was cautioned not to linger after dark.

And there was *Maimouna* at the end of Pesach, in Sacher Park—the Moroccans' large families, the boom of their music, indistinguishable to me from Arabic music, the people, indistinguishable from Arabs, and therefore at my periphery, even though the culture I loved so much was theirs.

When I was in Jerusalem, in 1974, Israel was a patched-together place of high ideals and practices that can only be called racist. At that professor's house in *Emek Refaim* ("valley of ghosts," the former German Colony), where I met the grandson of Martin Buber strumming his guitar, I also heard a Brandeis colleague's brother speaking hotly in defense of "settlement," jutting out his small brash beard and gesturing with the bowl of his too-perfect pipe, *the Land is ours*, and as it fell out the army chose not to evict the earliest settlements, hastily put together on a small West Bank hill by *Gush Emunim*, the "faithful" ones.

And when I was in Jerusalem my mother came to visit. She spoke Yiddish to the taxi driver and he understood her. That had felt strange, even wrong, somehow.

My mother was younger then than I am now. Here's how I always do the math:
In 1989, when she died of lung cancer, she was 69 years old.
So in 1974 she was 54, and so incredibly old to me.

I should have known that she would visit, because she was still fairly newly divorced and (at this point) had some money, and had never traveled on her own (though she had been to Portugal and maybe to Mexico with women friends); her plans were to spend time in Israel with me and then fly back through Rome. And: she kept a little diary of the trip, in a pocket-sized, spiral-bound "memo book" (made in Chattanooga, TN—not China), that cost 29 cents. The diary starts with suggestions her friends made for places to shop around Israel, as well as people to look up:
Helen Sutin father's brother lived near Netanya.
Lee Koren's cousin 'Yerna' lived in Kfar Saba,
and so on.

And the second half of the notebook is filled with names of people she met, couples and single women, Americans from all over Florida and a few Israelis (including the bus driver on one of her tours). There are also lots of names and addresses of family and friends, for sending home postcards.

My mother's diary—which runs from October 3rd to 20th, including a few days in Rome at the end of the trip—is mostly a chronology of flights, people met, meals eaten, and whatever she and I did together, written in her familiar cursive flourish. It's a travel journal, so I shouldn't feel disappointed that when I enter it, hoping to learn something new about my mother, I'm kept at a distance most of the time. She is tired a lot and records her naps (and why shouldn't she be tired? —I scold myself, exasperated).

Mrs. Perry made tea for us, delicious cake and conversation for about 2 hrs.

Here, I can hear my own voice echo—for I had sketched this same scene, years later: *She served it British-style, cream first in the cup.*

We were on the balcony and it was shaded.
I had an agonizing crush on Mrs. Perry's 18-year-old son, who was going into the army.

Went with Merle around 8 pm to take a walk. The streets are very crowded with young people…. Stopped at a vegetarian place—cheese omelets—Merle had eggplant salad—didn't like the way it looked. Left around 10 pm. Will see her tomorrow.

Well, here's something—not surprising, but indicative of her situation, maybe even her feelings:

Stopped in the [hotel bar] for a drink—Scotch...now I shall go to my room and drink my own scotch. —This place sure isn't a single's place—all couples (my age and older—very few younger—but all couples). Tomorrow maybe I'll see some historic places—and possibly change hotels.

Another echo:

How many times did I write in my own journals, but with an aggrieved tone, a real sense of complaint—about all the "couples" that surrounded me, during my long love-drought after I left my own marriage? (I always say I left it, to distinguish myself from my mother, the one who got left, who wanted my father back even when I was relieved he was gone.)

Mishaneh makom, mishaneh mazal—an Israeli saying I'd learned, means: "Change your place, change your luck"—and my mother did change hotels in Jerusalem, though I'm not sure her luck changed. My father remarried reflexively, compulsively, four times after leaving her, but remarry?—she never did.

—But who am I to say?

I mean, about her luck.

There is at least one photo of her with a man, holding hands, on some other trip—Caribbean travel? Or was that the one to Portugal?

Why shouldn't my mother have her own secrets? —And why should remarrying be the requisite characteristic of a successfully divorced woman? Many years, I saw her through

1970s eyes: of the neighbors, the relatives, hushed talk, her weight loss, the angst, the isolation (even though divorce, factually, was quite common in the '70s).

Maybe I saw her through her own eyes. She was lonely at times; her life was not easy.

But it was hers.

What I can see right now is that my mother betrayed no anxiety in her travel diary (the way I dramatically did, very often, in my own journals), despite airlines going on strike, having to change flights, arriving in Rome a day late (and *a nice young Italian couple* helped get her on a bus to the center of Rome, where her hotel was). A bus to the center of Rome! She knew no Italian. And I doubt that English was as rampant in Rome then, in October 1974, as it probably is now. She was traveling alone.

And yet, as she traveled, I think it meant opportunity to her, to meet new people—to make friends. Alone with her thoughts, she certainly didn't feel the need to write them down.

But she made lists of all the names, phone numbers, street addresses; that's what kept her company.

And yet—
a woman alone—drinking half a bottle of wine or more in a "nice" restaurant.
Even noting down those moments, before the entrée arrived: she was looking into the mirror of her own words.

I think she liked what she saw.

In my Jerusalem journal, I interrupted something else I'd been writing to note:
My mother is a good person.

And wrote nothing else about our time together.

*

As for Jerusalem: there's plenty more to write. A good Jewish daughter of diaspora, I had learned there were two cities: *Yerushalayim l'ma'alah*—the heavenly Jerusalem—and *Yerushalayim l'ma'ta*—its physical incarnation. Before I was on the scene to be initiated into the romance of ruins, I still imagined "belonging" there. And despite the masculine brusqueness of all Israelis, "my" Jerusalem—in retrospect—was female: hidden by veils, wearing long skirts or a bride's dress or an army uniform, but always a woman, as I was becoming a woman, drawn up out of my girlishness, and the city spoke Hebrew to me with multiple women's voices.

Before I ever went to Israel, I'd already developed a habit:
Nights or even fall afternoons at Brandeis, I would lock myself into a "listening room" in the basement of the library, with albums by The Ofarim—in English, "The Fawns"—a young Israeli singing duo hip enough to have been featured on the Smothers Brothers Show.

The friend I'd later make in Israel in 1975, my roommate Dorit, would mock their songs as "*shirey hoho*" meaning—what?—songs of the "Ho! Ho!" of soldiers on the march? The songs did drip with myth, patriotic invocations of The Land, of young men lost to the sudden violence of Arabs who simply did not understand the *purity* of fighting for a Jewish state in the aftermath of the Holocaust—
My land, my land...until I die.

Esther Ofarim's voice, supple and full, as if the swinging '60s lounge singer, Eydie Gormé, had instead sung Hebrew poetry set to folk music (Eydie and her husband Steve.... They were Jewish, too, my parents liked them).

It was a woman's voice, then, that seduced me into a yearning for Israel.

And my professor of Hebrew, Ariella Goldberg, also had something to do with it. Ariella with her smoky, cigarette-inflected voice.

She was tall and thin and bony, her face always animated, under lanky hair. She was Israeli, and therefore beautiful. Chain-smoking outside of class; long scarves, boots—elegant and sinewy at the same time. She was tall, I think. And the language she spoke was magical, fluted, lyrical. I wanted to possess this language that stained rocks in the land of milk and honey. Ariella, a name both pretty and tough (*ari* is Hebrew for lion).

Fall 1973, Brandeis

On a placid afternoon in early November, leaves falling past the tall, cold windows, a rift opened in the classroom air, and we could peer inside it and see thousands of miles away. "Look," she says, "you've never seen this"—and spreads out the tissue-paper of the international edition of *Ma'ariv*, one of the Israeli daily newspapers. We gather around her desk. Amid the wispy rustling papers, we see pairs of little photos, accompanied by the biblical quote: *THEY WERE PLEASANT AND LOVING IN THEIR LIVES, AND IN THEIR DEATHS THEY WERE NOT PARTED.* These were pictures of just the *brothers* who'd been killed in the so-called Yom Kippur War. The losses had affected almost every family in the country.

Ha kol b'ivrit, everything in Hebrew, of course, as she continues, "Look, this one was 19. Look at that one, his face, such a *yeled*, a boy"—In mid-sentence, turns on her heel and walks out.

Was she crying? Ariella?

After a few minutes she returns, composed once again.
"I didn't know how else to tell you."

How do they print on paper so fine?

She folded the pleasant faces into each other, all evenly silver and black and evenly smiling, pressed them into a book and continued the class.

I didn't learn until 2000 that in 1985, just ten years after my junior year in Jerusalem, Ariella had died of breast cancer. She was not quite 50.

I found this out because I'd wound up buying a short novel she'd written, under her maiden name of "Deem," published in English by the Jewish Publication Society (translation by Nelly Segal) in 1987. On the back cover is a lovely photo of her with a bio underneath, that ends with her death. The book's English title is *Jerusalem Plays Hide and Seek*. When I was one of her students in 1973-74 at Brandeis, she must have been working on her novel, because it was published in its original Hebrew in 1976 in Tel Aviv.

This means that the year when I was studying in Jerusalem, Ariella had been writing about her relationship to that city, in stories inspired by a box of heavy glass slides she had bought in a Boston antique shop. The images are reproduced in the book and reveal aspects of Jerusalem and its environs dating back to the late 19th century. The empty beauty of the landscape (the Mount of Olives, the Valley of Kidron, the Judaean hills) stirs up memories of "my" city—post-occupation, yet before the intense colonization of the West Bank.

When I open the book now, quickly read parts of it, I'm drawn back—
in Jerusalem again, but in *her* long-ago city, and in the long, long ago she describes through quirky, shifting narrative (veils dropping and being removed), characters who came to life for her through her poring over the glass slides.

At one point we nearly intersect—*In the morning, I had a cup of coffee at Café Savion in Rehavia* (p. 92)—the same café that I wrote about in 1978, in an article for a Boston

Jewish newspaper, *genesis 2*, lifted (I note in the article), from my journal:

One night I decided I could not live without a piece of chocolate cake, and so I dragged Dorit with me on a late stroll through lush spring stillness. The café was a short way from our apartment building up the hill and through the square, past various embassies and notables' houses, their stone all watered with streetlight. And a block before Savion was Rabin's house...

And—
I come across a journal entry now that refers to a forgotten time at Ariella's house, where apparently she would sometimes host Brandeis students, for an afternoon or evening class. I rely on my journal to remember:

3/21/74
Class at Ariella's was so good—sitting around the long dining room table, sipping sub-tly-spiced tea & eating chocolate cookies, speaking (trying to) in Hebrew—house full of musical instruments, hand-made drawings, carvings, paintings; old things—a huge Tanach with commentary <u>censored</u> in 17th century Italy (it was Ariella's father's) (is she Italian? Sfardi?)—Russian icon—clay oil lamps—sequoia pine cone...

And in *Jerusalem Plays Hide and Seek*, I find, to my surprise:

At the end of [summer], I returned to my home in Boston. Autumn arrived, and I returned to my work and my students at Brandeis.

All through that autumn and the winter that followed, I nursed the pictures and scenes in my heart anxiously, longingly, hungrily. With the coming of spring, I rented an old-fashioned projector. I bought a large cake, some cookies, a large can of coffee, and some fancy paper napkins. And I invited my students to come to my house on Saturday night for 'an evening of slides and coffee'.... (pp. 125-26).

That must not have been the evening I remembered in my journal.
It must've been another class. We drank tea; there were no slides.

Ariella had also been on the committee that interviewed students for the Hiatt Program in Israel, and I was convinced even back then that her recommendation got me in.

If she had lived...what would have happened? As it is, I discover she wrote another novel, *After You, Benjamin*, that has not been translated into English, as well as literary criticism. There is also an untranslated volume of essays that celebrates her as a writer. Really, it's not until now—after graduate school in English, after my dissertation, after teaching my own college students for years—that I can open her book and read it the way it deserves to be read, recognizing its poetry and surreality (laughing, self-aware)—its moves, gestures.... I should revive my knowledge of Hebrew, I should research her, translate her! She is a boon companion, as a writer.

Considering the thinness of my Hebrew, this is fantasy. Instead, I search for her husband Eddie online. I remember him, with his mustache and jaunty hat, and their two milky-skinned daughters, with long, white-blonde hair, the weight of fleece. I don't remember how it happened, but I know that on a Shabbat or a Jewish holiday I was walking with them on campus, and they even came with me to my dorm room in "the Castle," a grim structure that, from the outside, looked like a fairy tale, though entirely institutional from within. —And in 2000, I'd found him on a listserv and written to him. I have two emails from him, printed out (of course), in the Archive.

—But it's 20 years later, and I can't find him. If he'd been exactly Ariella's age, he'd be in his mid-80s by now. Has he passed away?

With clues from his past emails, I find their older daughter, who is a scholar of classical literature and part of the faculty at Hebrew University in Jerusalem. In one online photo, she looks a lot like her mother. She is married to the son of a famous Israeli writer. She has a daughter named Ariella, who is herself, now, likely married with children...

This is simply how it works:
People grow up, have children, age, and die.

In my own world-variant, "growing up" lasts forever (there are no children), and Ariella survives: language-giver; writer.

*

It's 2010, in Louisville, KY, where I am five years into living with my cat in an apartment that needs a paint job—after my divorce.

By now I have forgotten Jerusalem.

It's receded under the weight of the mundane, the everyday assimilation of self into place.

Home accrues over time despite the inner drama, the curdling expectations, the self-righteous desire. You set your clock, direct your compass, gather items for the journey, keep searching the horizon and all the time you're sinking deeper, deeper into routine: gradually familiarity has overwhelmed you, and you never noticed.

Like the train that rattles my second-floor flat countless times each day and night, reduced now to a bare
notation: that sound,
that's <u>train</u>—going by.

Will I ever even leave this apartment?

The woman who lived in the downstairs unit wound up staying twenty years: then, in a fit of last-minute-nearing-sixty angst, hurled herself toward a country purchase—a house she stumbled on that fit the cut of her most ancient dreams.

So, maybe I'll move to Jerusalem?

Never, never, a chorus of nevers

HOME AS OTHER

It's 1988. On a January afternoon lit from a great distance by a wasted sun, glowering like a chunk of old yellow ice, I retrace the way I used to walk, when I lived here in the '70s. The wind burns across the surface of the Empire State Mall, picking up an added chill from the veined marble of the fleshless buildings.

I've flown in from California, to visit my mother. She's home recuperating after a short stint in Memorial Hospital. Tests had been performed, her blood tapped more regularly than trees at maple syrup time. A shadow had been glimpsed along her spine, stealing in among the vertebrae. For one happy day they'd pronounced it a slipped disc. Then the doctors put their heads together and come up with a more profound diagnosis: *it* was back.

Home is now a two-room "senior apartment" in a tower 10 stories tall, to the north of Albany. Last night we sat in the living room with curtains open so we could watch a changing patch of sky. Planes headed for the airport swooped in over the tower; this was the point in their flight where they hit the brakes before landing, so the sound of their engines changed. With every set of pulsating lights drawing closer out of the night sky, my mother said, "Ooooh, there's another one, there's another one!" as if she'd never seen planes land before in her life.

Today I want to walk and walk in the places that once felt like home to me.

"Did the poor little kitten lose her mittens?" Her voice sounds sleepy. I stand in the State Capitol building, at the pay phone in an old-fashioned booth, and look out to see my mittens being swept up by a custodian from the place where I'd carelessly dropped them. "Just a minute Mom!" —I go to retrieve them. By the time I'm back on the line, I realize my mother isn't sleepy, she's just dopey. It's the morphine for her pain, which was growing in a rigid tree inside her back. "I'll be on the bus soon," I lie.

Here are the forbidden words: death; dying; cancer. Everything else is permissible. It's amazing, this being so, how small the scope of conversation remains, sitting with my mother. As if we're in a darkened room with only a flashlight's circle of unrelenting light, focused on a tabletop. Inside the circle are the things we can discuss: Glen's arthritic hip, Sid's tax business, Ellen's children, bridge with the girls, where Gloria should clean, what to have for dinner (and who will pay for it). Safe topics, things of permanence in a world made shifty and strangely indeterminate.

*

Perhaps it's not surprising that Jim and I met in the spring of 1988. It was during a period when people wrote letters to one another via a PO Box at the San Francisco Bay Guardian. It turned out that he was a near neighbor to where I was living in North Oakland at that time, and things went on from there. He was a good person, stable, just beginning his career as a journalist. Two years later we got married.

For years, even after the divorce, people would comment on what a lovely event it had been—in Cragmont Park in the Berkeley Hills, on a day in August when August did not yet mean fire season. There were benedictions in the ancient Hebrew, as well as a famous passage about love from the New Testament (Jim was not Jewish) and a love-struck look from bride to groom (there's photographic evidence).

At one point during the ceremony, a couple of rock climbers emerged at the lip of the park, then hastened away.

Post-ceremony, post-honeymoon (which had been in northern Montana, exceedingly beautiful and foreign to the Jewish bride), we made our home first in one apartment, then another, because the thought of buying "into" Berkeley felt impossible to me. Because I didn't want to "settle down" so far away from the East Coast—which I see now, felt like home mainly because it was thousands of miles away, and unobtainable.

Home as *other*.

In summer 2002, we buy a house (no, Jim buys it, with a down-payment from his father) —not in Berkeley, but in Louisville, where we had moved in the waning moments of the century (Jim got a job at a venerable newspaper; I was writing my dissertation).

Two years after that, you will get your job as a professor, working full-time at a small down-town university with a long Catholic history (home as other).

One year after that, you leave the marriage.

July 2002, Louisville

The night after we move into the house on North Bellaire, Jim has a conference, so he's away, and there's a bad storm, and I'm afraid to sleep in the house alone. In my absence, our two cats apparently go crazy. When I come back in the morning, curtains have been pulled down, cat fur's settling in the middle of the living room floor, and Lucy-cat is cowering in an upstairs closet that smells of urine. Her eyes have a pinkish glow. The attic door, blown open.

I'm convinced the place is haunted.

And it is: a plastic letter, "M," emerges from under the refrigerator; a piece of striped candy. A towel with a goose stitched on it, from the top of the kitchen cabinets. That's one layer of prior life, in our house, the family who left in a quick weekend, taking their gingham curtains from the windows and modest brown crosses from the walls.

Every creak in this house registers; every sigh inside the walls, every suggestion of age, settling; an imperfect history, staining the edges, or littering those strange, grilled vacancies in the floor—the "air returns"—where, when you look down in, you see: a plastic toy soldier (the kind that comes in a cereal box); a marble; somebody's Kleenex; bits and twists of paper; other things, indistinguishable, ground to dust.

The family who sold us this house lived here happily it seems. Toddler Claire slept in the room that we repainted and now sleep in ourselves. Baby Emily slept in the room Jim's taken for his office. And the parents slept—here, right here where I've set up my computer, that's where they had their fertile bed.

146

But all I see are: windows stuck shut, their interstices filled with putty to prevent air seepage, further preventing their being yanked open. Window trim stained a bleak, dark mahogany, seeming to fade by dint of sunlight. Places where the trim along the base of the walls is coming off, exposing dust-filled holes. Varnish peeling off pine floors, like sticky dark honey that's been eaten away.

My face, grim in the mirror after another night of not being able to sleep. How one can look like a mess of shadows, it's as if they were always there, but the skin—the opposite of translucent—*transdark*—lets them peer through. Imperfection. Stubbornness. Fatigue.

The ice-maker downstairs kicks into gear, a faint sound of internal thunder; I jump. Air ducts, tucked beneath the floorboards among the pipes, gently swell and contract, and I feel them, under my own skin.

It was not supposed to be like this, so shabby and sagging.

And two mismatched adults, trying harder to find their way separately than together.

    —Archival note: *House of the unmaking of your marriage.*

Refugees

In 2002, in Louisville, you also had a part-time job at Catholic Charities teaching adult refugees "college preparation English"—a catch-all title for encouraging them to read at a high school level and to get comfortable with the American cultural obsession of writing clear, linear prose, as well as your own obsession—*self-expression*.

You met in the classroom of an old Catholic School with peeling ceilings and cracked linoleum floors; the dust of many generations of tired and perhaps bored students drifting around you. Night after night you met, at the end of their long work days on assembly lines or in packaging. They sat wearily yet attentive. They were exploring the mystery of becoming American.

Back then, you wrote:

> *This intensely hot week, I try to take my students to Alaska. That is, have them—the Cubans & Sudanese—read from John Haines' 1989 memoir, <u>The Stars, the Snow, the Fire: Twenty-five Years in the Northern Wilderness</u>, invoking snow, thirty-below, and darkness that never quite peels off your hide. They struggle gamely with the words: "lynx" "axe" "spruce" "firebox" "kindling". What a selfish game, because it's really for me, this reading (on a day of 80 percent humidity and skies overcast with car exhaust, when walking means moving languidly and still collecting drips down the insides of both thighs); I'm trying to get far away from here, as far from my life as possible.*

Haines says: "How many winters have gone by like this? Each morning that begins in the same quiet way...." —and I envy him the continuity. The repeated memories, each layer dropped on like an icy glaze, thickening, rich.

In another place he says: "As I stand here, refreshed by the stillness and closeness of the night, I think it is a good way to live." It's where "the books he reads" are stars, snow, fire. Where he seems to dwell amid simple universals of primitive life: hauling wood from the pile, removing an animal's body from a bloody snare and shearing off the furry hide, making things from every piece of meat, skin, bone. A life as fantastic to me as anything that might exist on another planet—though I don't really want that raw, crude, life, or imagine I miss it, here in my envelope of electric ease.

What I miss—I mean, feel the lack of, in a deep, wounding sense—is a skill he has, that he passes lightly over in a paragraph: "I remember things. Names, friends of years past, a wife far off. Last week I saw a magazine article on contemporary painters in NYC, photographs of people I once knew...all that seems very far and ages distant."

... "My life is here, in this country I have made, in the things I have built.... I do not want more than this."

—He remembers: but he does not cling, he does not long, he has let go. He acknowledges distance; he recognizes that time has moved him, like an ivory chess piece, someplace outside the imagination, even, of the people in those New York City photographs, and he accepts it.

He does more than accept: he acknowledges that his life is "here:" in "country" and "things" that he, out of his own fervent imaginings and manual labor, has "made." And that satisfies him.

It's as if he is present for the present moments of his life, and does not need to haul around sacks of old letters, does not need to maintain all the filaments reaching back to a complicated past.

The only threads he mentions are those of heavy flax, which he uses to sew collar seams for a harness made from moose leather.

But I still feel the pang: of things I want to unload, of histories I'd like to be rid of; the desire not to cling or hoard but to learn how to shed

(rise up from buckled legs in a damp clearing, sniff the air and be off—everything glistening and new).

*

The odd thing, of course—the irony—is that your students had all, by dint of political circumstance, been forced to abandon whole chunks of their pasts, had not been allowed to take more than a suitcase with them, in their flight. And their writing was filled with details, conscious and unconscious, of the damage—of roots dangling, hungry for soil—

of an earth still large enough, despite globalization, to encompass distances that seemed final. (*Were* final, for the Somalis, the Afghanis, the Iraqis...)

Home as other...

You had read about people like your students in the newspapers; you had even published poems about people like them, back in California. Now the subjects of your poems had taken actual form and sat in your classroom, struggling with pronouns and verb tenses, and you intermixed your own feelings with theirs, as if you could really feel as they did.

What caught you (thank goodness), prevented you from immersing in that assumption was the reality of their presence. It punctured your fantasy of ever really comprehending what they had gone through. The contradiction: attempting to give them access, through language, to a larger culture (in the U.S.); and the impossibility of their conveying to an American, in these second-hand words, their lived experiences.

But meeting these individuals and being their "Teacher" (as they called you with affection and respect) has never left you. The Archive contains scraps of their writing. From Yakov, a young Sudanese man who wrote: *i am alonely*. He was far from his family, a huge family, his friends...many of them probably dead, his community destroyed.

I miss my country, Iran…. i want to go back. Khadija had one subject, and her spelling was guesswork, and she mixed up present and past, but the meat of her heart was there, on the page, where she also described being so busy from when she wakes up till class time till bedtime and then the alarm and it starts all over again.

Your students embodied horrible facts; they were walking storehouses of historical event.

You wrote:

> *Their suffering means something—I swear it does—part of a universal grammar that also includes, in other countries, at other moments islanded in time, embodiments of profoundest love and trust.*

> *There is a language I am trying to teach myself, in teaching them vocabulary for writing their own stories.*

It is a language I can no longer remember.

*

"Have you ever...?"

Once the exercise begins, you don't know what will emerge. "Have you ever...saved someone's life?" "Have you ever...seen a ghost?"

It was fall again. A young Bosnian woman who worked full-time in a bank and had a husband who worked third shift and a young daughter, arrived punctually every evening, after having gone home to cook dinner for her small family. Samira was blonde with marble-blue eyes, and she talked about the customs associated with observing Ramadan in Bosnia: her mother the first to get up at 4 in the morning to cook a big breakfast, something to sustain them until evening, and they all had to eat before first light, because once the sun is up, the fast begins again, renewed daily. She made you see Ramadan in a new way—as families, sleepily sitting in kitchens all over the world, a special time in the still-dark, eating food prepared with love to give them strength, to fulfill what their prophet has asked them to do...

Back to the exercise. A fellow student continued: "Have you ever thought...you were going to die?"—and Samira started scribbling intensely on a piece of notebook paper. What she started writing that evening eventually became an article in the school newspaper. *"I did—it was the spring war broke out in my country..."*

You all listened to her read her story, absorbed and silent. At the end, when tears sprang to her eyes—not about the war, the crack of guns, the hiding, the hunger, but about being there in Louisville, never having imagined she would ever feel so safe again—another student (one from Haiti) put his hand lightly on her shoulder and asked if he could finish reading it for her.

<u>Spring 2003: The Information</u>

On a rainy spring afternoon, pausing in her chores, a married woman in her late 40s imagines seeing the faces of old boyfriends on the TV screen.

She stands with her back to the TV, facing the living room picture window—but obliquely, so the TV's reflection will register in it—holding the clicker behind her back and running channels, pausing about a second (if that) on each. Images continually surface, forming a pleasing river of large blank faces with mouths crinkling and opening and closing (the TV always on mute); maybe one of them is the Israeli soldier who grew up on a kibbutz, or the sensitive child psychologist who was narcissistic in bed, both handsome, defiled, strange.

The man she's married to comes home tired and preoccupied on a daily basis. They cook dinner in segments (he does the meat, she does the vegetables) and eat in separate rooms connected by a vacancy, framed by pocket doors. She's sorry for the circles under his eyes; she knows he works hard, writing the news stories that fill papers in the morning (that fewer and fewer people read, the revenues declining). The news keeps him in a trance; but hypnotized, he does not realize his condition and thus carries on, going to work every morning to write columns of words, to fill up the paper with news, which is no longer new by the time it appears the next morning....

There are always new bits of information, undifferentiated, streaming, to absorb. What she takes for granted, by now: nothing exists that cannot be made into the tag line of an ad campaign. Further, no matter how painful a snippet of news or even how devastating, nothing happens that cannot be instantly embedded in a stream of chirpy how-to stories: "scientists alarmed by decreases in bird species" followed by "be your own money coach!" followed by "suicide bombers strike in Jerusalem" followed by "your child can learn while sleeping!" and "springtime fashions call for dazzle!" Sometimes, startled by a particularly blatant incongruity, she struggles to—what was that, that thing she needed so badly to remember? Perhaps it's just a chemical that creates that feeling of need—to remember something.

Memory has its place, but you can't count on it. Fickle friend. It's better to focus on what the hydra-heads of the media and the internet offer, the teeth-brighteners, tummy-tucks, passion for the flag, disdain for history, adoration of the Father, the Son, the....

Addiction to the images, to the scroll, is draining, but a part of everyday life. You accept and keep your head down. You try to clear a narrow space, an interiority the messages, the images cannot penetrate.

Now, say it's 2019. Can anyone remember the clubbing of baby seals? Aung San Suu Kyi before the Rohingya genocide, still confined to her modest house in Burma? —and there are always young men with phantom pain after the detonation of a leg, an arm, teenage girls forced to give birth, racehorses converted to tinned meat, but who remembers the way they asked the flight attendant: "Are you sure?" when she reported the hijackers, the way they refused to believe her, minutes before the first plane hit the towers?

—Just part of the information we once carried...

The TV is still on, like a large bald eye that, unseeing, projects what it imagines into the room: money, waste, lies, unearned sentiment. Perhaps it would be better to live moored in isolation: like a Brontë sister scribbling away with icy hands, a time before trains, a time when even letters arrived slowly, and when someone left for another country, you knew you'd never see him again in the flesh.

—But then there would have been no California, no possibility of getting there, paradisical strip of green on a rugged coast, your first night there waking to the bed's unmistakable movement, your roommate's mysterious smile: "just mamma rocking the cradle;" there would have been no flight, no way to reach it and return, it would be a dream, a postcard someone sent.

Memory still has a place in the scheme of things, because its density helps anchor you, because the flash of an earring in someone's curls can bring back a whole other life, possibly your own.
There is a place called California and it holds a third of your life.

To be a figure inserted in its landscape was once enough.

July 2020, Bloomington

Millions of stories, billions of them.

Why *this* story? Of the once-girl, now-woman on her way to being "old"?

I was a hidden treasure, and I loved to be known.

This is a "hadith," a saying of Muhammad, and as I write this I know little about Muhammad and less about the place of hadiths in Islamic mysticism. But this utterance of the Divine has captured my heart.

A fellow student in an online course on "self-knowledge" under the umbrella of Beshara, a spiritual community organized around self-discovery, says of this hadith: "When I read this, it is my own I, inside the universal I—they are the same." Since the Beshara community is engaged with what has been called "non-duality," this student's interpretation is not blasphemous.

Perhaps that is why *this* life, this story, has any significance at all.

WRITING CALIFORNIA

Always "going back" to California...

February 2010: One Return

Large rectangles of clear sky, viewed through a living room window in the Berkeley hills, or through a skylight in a bathroom in San Francisco.

The sky unfolds itself in an elegant sequence of mathematical formulae that no one understands or needs to.

The sky, so uncontainable, burns itself up in a scintillating panorama of interstitial colors (and at night, the values change).

The sky unchains everyone who looks deeply into it.

The sky and the ocean belong together, it's hard to tell which is which, each bathes in the other.

The city fills with a mind-numbing series of people moving along momentary paths and crowding any vista.

—I don't know where I am, why am I here?

I used to work in that building in my 30s.
I used to climb these hills with a sense of future triumph.
Now, I am visiting from that future.

Once from a high-up path on Russian Hill, I saw way down, out there in the Bay, a
moving piece of red licorice (a ship).

What color's the Golden Gate Bridge painted? (Hint: It's not gold.)

So many tattoos, so many lesbian couples, so many freshly published books, so many
alluring racks of cookies.

On this visit, I eat four kinds of folded food:
a crepe, a dosha, a knish, a mu shu pancake.

I eat cramped up on a too-tall bar stool (twice); in a booth; on a bench with tiny ants,
on a dune scrabby with grass; in Dolores Park; hurrying along, on Mission Street.

No matter what, it tasted good: creamy, sharp, tangy, sweet, crumbly, dense, moist,
salty, crunchy.

1982, 455 61st St.: First Arrival

The kitchen had a wooden table shaped like a kidney. Or maybe—just a curve.
A pale avocado green, dinged, scratched, a fading relic of past glory.

Avocados: a line of plastic cups along the kitchen windowsill, each with a pit supported
by—toothpicks? (The memory is dreamily unclear.) Each an avocado plant at egg stage,
lit by warm dusty air.

Pots: aluminum, banged up.

Stove: electric.

Ants: fetching crumbs in erratic lines, on cracked linoleum floor, counters, table.

Roommates: five, three, four in number.

Once upon a time, I lived there:
where the sun falls into the ocean, *plop*, night after night, its flame extinguished by the
Pacific (which I did not witness directly but knew was happening, after the sky turned
its lilac, lime and pink, which spelled *WEST* and the farthest boundary to the country,
beyond which no one could go except for by sea).[16]

---

[16] The weather satellite simply called WEST.... Remember the night the forecaster joked about its having
been lost, gone off the edge of an invisible map? Satellite WEST had gone west.

In North Oakland, on 61st St. off Telegraph, next to the run-down clapboard church where a family lived whose son had recently been arrested for rape—the house to which the above-described kitchen belonged, my first California home, was built of painted particleboard, inside and out, with a thin felt of carpet, smudged linoleum, walls to whisper through, tacky plastic insert around the bathtub. Skylights in upstairs bedrooms, sliding glass doors on makeshift balconies...when Pacific winds hurled down rain, my breasts swelled, hurt.

From age 28 to 46: California.
Everything, registering in the body...

A needle aspiration revealed—nothing, only micro-calcifications, very common among women. Still, fear of cancer, so: miso soup every morning, brown rice and aduki beans, slowly chewing seaweed (so spiritual), dipping into pottery bowls.... Most days I walked past Zachary's, a place serving deep-dish pizza (so many no-nos: dairy, white flour). I concentrated on the deep green of vegetation, picturing kale everywhere.

> Years later, when I was diagnosed with "stage zero" ductal carcinoma—DCIS, as it's known in the trade—a beloved California friend, a fellow poet, suggested that breasts had to do with love and perhaps I was blocked there (and the ovarian cancer she eventually died of—I thought perhaps, but never told her, it had to do with her fierce grip on career—but we all have our own way of defining, under-standing what befalls us).

I had always been afraid of breast cancer.
I never did want children.
Was there a connection? I ate popcorn to cheer myself up when all around me friends were eating ice cream (the ultimate macrobiotic sin: dairy and too cold!).

—And later, one summer in San Francisco sleeping on a single mattress in a redeemed closet (i.e., with a window in it), something I had done before, back in Somerville, 1977—the only room available. I didn't care. So what if I was 30? My stomach: anxiety held it in against my spine, breathing always somewhat hampered.

Yosemite, my favorite place on earth back then, meant the soles of my feet. Walking from the tents of would-be mountaineers and staff adjacent to Curry Village, on pine cones and crunchy shrub, walking in the Valley, feet splaying painfully inside my too-comfortable moccasins—back in Oakland, I was prescribed orthotics.

And later, after 61ˢᵗ St. (where I'd spent three years):

Cloaca:
A musical word, non-musical meaning:
A common passageway for feces, urine and reproduction [in the human embryo]...which eventually transforms into the rectum, bladder, and genitalia..."[17]

---

[17] https://www.rxlist.com/cloaca/definition.htm

That was at 35, on a thin path toward getting married.

Jim and I already lived together, in a third floor apartment a short walk from Piedmont Avenue.

It was a beautiful flat, shining wood floors, Moorish windows, but small.

So much anxiety and terror—before the wedding.

I couldn't let go.

I needed a sphincterotomy.

But other layers, parts, get involved—in the cell turnover, in the layering of experience.

Once upon a time (begin again), a woman in her late 20s and still untethered, always on the verge and never actually arriving anywhere—

The Berkeley poet Lyn Hejinian, whose work I wouldn't read for another decade, discusses "open" and "closed" texts in her 1983 essay, "The Rejection of Closure," and alights on writing's infinitude.... She writes:

The "open text," by definition, is open to the world and particularly to the reader.... It speaks for writing that is generative rather than directive. The writer relinquishes total control and challenges authority as a principle and control as a motive. The "open text" often emphasizes or foregrounds process...and thus resists the cultural tendencies that seek to identify and fix material and turn it into a product; that is, it resists reduction and commodification.[18]

---

[18] From Hejinian's essay, as posted on the Poetry Foundation website. https://www.poetryfoundation. org/articles/69401/the-rejection-of-closure

Writing and life (especially in my 20s) echoed each other in my own self-reading, resisting "cultural tendencies" such as accumulation of wealth or concomitant creation of family.

When I arrived in Oakland in 1982, it was during the time of "yuppies," the rapid minting of wealthy young professional couples. I would walk up North Street to Colby and left to 62nd (or was it 63rd?) and up to College, because it was on those streets that the most beautiful houses were arrayed, each a different pastel color, with careful bungalowed shingles and weeping wisteria or explosions of bougainvillea draped down walls or trellises or over garden gates. What was it like to live in this house or that one? The well-fed children at scrubbed plank tables; the adults with their briefcases, sharp-edged suits and Volvos, the men, the women, alike in their business dress and intensity, the laser focus on improving the lives of their innocent offspring.

What was it like? To have the money to live that kind of life.

But why live it? —If I could enjoy the ease of being low on the food chain, in a collective house with a chore wheel, volunteer hours at the food co-op, and a part-time job. The first dot.com boom had yet to happen. My rent was—what—50 dollars a month? And there was still an open field where an expensive food emporium was later built (we called it "Mark-up"—instead of "Market"—Hall).

Why walk when you can glide, run down escalator stairs to the open door of a BART train, waiting to take you across the Bay?

Oh, California—so altered now!—but then, an excellent place for a wandering poet,
because it always verged on water and air—
an opus of possibilities (hovering briefly between the light of day and nothing) over
　　unmediated ocean.

From the Archive: a True Story

It's that first winter in California, and rain is pounding the delicate frame of the slap-
dash house in which they all live: glorified cabin, walls and roof a single board thick,
skylights that leak, the cheapest carpet available tacked to plywood floors, a smell of
mold clouding the A-frame rafters:

Here they make a home, M and her roommates (who are all active in CISPES, the
Committee in Solidarity with the People of El Salvador; who are constantly at meetings
where they issue statements, revise them and issue them again). Each bedroom with a
tiny redwood balcony accessible by sliding glass doors that stick (but are also tempting
to thieves); M covers hers with an Indian bedspread, too lazy to make a drape.

Here they live, and in M's room she's created a bed from a wood plank and a skinny
used mattress, perched on plastic milk crates; and her dresser is made of a leaf to a long-
lost table, also set on plastic crates, and she has to kneel to gaze into the mirror; and an
unsteady card table serves as a desk, and when she types it shudders along. At night one
roommate taps M's door and enters, forsaking his own messy room that smells of dirty

laundry and grass, with its portrait of Che staring down on the damp bed: revolutionaries and love, something like that (when their phone *click-clicks*, they laugh about being tapped, which makes her feel part of a Bigger Thing, and even though she does nothing for CISPES, she's proud of it as she looks on).

—Yes it's him, the skinny bearded one with the big brown eyes, he smells like the pot he's been smoking, he's wearing long underwear and his shoulders are tense, he climbs under the sleeping bag she uses as a blanket, the house is freezing, another Pacific storm has unleashed its wind and rain, she clings to his knobby body like a wet leaf to a branch, it's blowing them into each other, it's blowing them farther away—

His limbs form a rough frame on which she drapes herself, a warm serape, a liquid tent, she covers his frail places, he guides her deeper into herself, a boat bumping up against a dock, and so to sleep.

*

On 61ˢᵗ St., I wrote:

radishes, at the full moon
I lift them from the earth straight into
my mouth

no I don't. That's for the
neighbors, tending their gardens

babies strapped
to their backs....

I'm 30 years old.   wading through life
w/an armful of books I don't
read, spending hours
stooped over adding machines typewriters   or   gazing
far into the green
field of a computer screen.   this
is my life.   no one's
wife, but my own
little girl

For my first full-time job, wearing thrift shop dresses and Chinese slippers, I race-walk to the place of casual carpool, where people line up in the morning fog and wait for this B'mer or that Volvo or Mercedes to pull up so we can enter, two at a time, to comprise the magic 3 that lets us take the diamond lane over the long bridge into San Francisco. One summer (my experience of "the City" having made me newly restless, and after a falling out with one of my housemates), I make the move to San Francisco, to the Mission District, just a few blocks from where I work. I occupy a room the size of a walk-in closet in a sprawling flat filled with internationals.

Wet dark streets in the Mission. On the run, late for a meeting.

Showroom of mirrors on Valencia, in which I always check my image as I walk by—
lunchtime away from my office building, the "Bayview"—the elevator there makes me
nervous, but the kind Latino janitor always says, "if it ever stops, just sit still, wait until
I come and get you."

A kind of hardness to that Valencia St.—newsprint glued to sidewalk with spit and dog
shit and pink gum and stink. The rawness of its arc, exposed to sky—
same wide sky connecting to Bridge, to Bay, to ocean on the city's other edge.

> —And the gay boys, the dancers who choreograph their own steps, and your pride
> that they know you by name (a daisy chain of lovers' arms and sickness and death
> —Joah and Teddy and James and beloved Charlie, he's the Pan you dance with in
> a shared artist collective, he's the one who pulls you to him in flushed confusion
> —yours, not his...).

But I have trouble falling asleep in my San Francisco foothold, and it's not just because
of the proverbial drunks shouting in the alley. Somehow the East Bay just feels more
like home—I have some *roots* there—and before long I find an apartment not far from
my old neighborhood, a studio I fill with collages and conceptual art (how about a min-
iature iron with tiny plastic babies glued to its surface?). A long walk down Piedmont
Avenue and I can stroll in the cemetery, which has a great view, and explore the colum-
barium at "Chapel of the Chimes."

And write:
my mother's shipping me a box of
plates, cups, spoons, dishes
It's real heavy, she warns me
(I'll need a man
to pick it up)

Helping me from 3000 miles away
when I should be in the house
next door, able to
lean over a fence
fetch a few things   Mom,
I really didn't mean it—moving away—

Don't you know I'll just
come back some day &
this stuff will go back into its crate—?
when I come back

Of course I didn't say those things out loud.
She was 65 and her apartment was shrinking around her, no room for service-for-six.

And by then I was 32, still a "girl"—who continued writing

—and come through the door in
a ten-year-old body,
filled w/horse spirits &
words, languages meant to be
spoken—when I'm back
to follow you around
your kitchen, puzzled

by your measurements of flour &
oven temperature, patting the
chicken breasts the way you'd
pat me on the bottom,
throwing them into the pan
to fry—When you grow up
& get married, you say
and fix me with a smile

After getting tired of living alone I wound up in another roommate situation, in a duplex just a few blocks from 61st St.

And that's where I lived when I met Jim, through the Bay Guardian personals.

1992: Flashforward, two years after marriage

The doctor I was seeing at Kaiser for the usual ills (IBS, anxiety, whatever kept me revolving through doctors' offices, especially if the fee was only five dollars, as it was back then) was hugely pregnant.
Between the exam table and the sink and cabinets, her belly filled space.

"Don't wait too long," she advised me. She was 40 and considered medically "elderly" for giving birth—but at least this was her second child.

"Right," I said, "Of course," I said, biting my lip and squinting at the ceiling light (flat on the table, prodded, poked).

But the MFA program I was now a part of was getting busier and so was Jim's job on the other side of the Caldecott tunnel.

Cars flowed over 580, a never ending night-time *shushhhhhhhhhhhh*. The sound followed us into sleep, on the black cherrywood bedstead that had belonged to Jim's parents, who had insisted we accept it, and despite the smallness of our bedroom and the ease with which I felt claustrophobic, my husband had echoed that insistence—it was a family heirloom, after all.

A marriage bed, a child bed…and in it I dreamed of a poetry that could say and do anything it pleased, charting its solitary and insistent course across my relatively unplanned life.

*

What can make you feel stable in a place like California, where the earth, uneasy, turns over in sleep? The tremors are constant; there's equipment sited in ditches and promising crevices, where the ground's movements have become more obvious over time—but you never feel them, at least, not as you walk or grocery shop or lie in bed next to a new lover. It must do something to one's psyche, though—the hundreds of microscopic movements, like whispers up through the feet and legs, through the cradling hips and into the heart. Unsteady ground, chewing off the roots of new plants, slowly.

Even back East, the oldest members of the family begin to tremble, weaken and fade, images in the heat-shimmer of September pavement.

Yet there, where buildings are constructed of brick, you don't have to move the framed picture that hangs above a bed; and you can actually track natural dangers on weather maps. It's where "disaster" is just what your uncle calls a particular nephew, in that Albany-sharp accentuated "a":
He's a disASter.

"Back home": where you *really* live, even after the first few years in California, the first decade and—beyond.

Starfish on the molten-wet beach, lacking an arm

—won't it grow back?

* * *

When I was a small child I had a comforting story I used to tell myself, on the way to sleep.

It had to do with a small wagon, the red kind that 1950s Dick & Jane children used, to pull their friends and toys in.

I didn't have such a wagon; I didn't even want one during my daily life. But in the wagon I imagined, half-dreamed in seamless nighttime breaths, was piled everything I needed:

food, of course (pizza appeared often, and a bottle of milk like the ones the milkman used to leave); cozy blankets and favorite toys, stuffed animals, plush, button-eyed. A tent covering on top to keep off the rain.

I could go anywhere with this wagon, just pulling it along. I'd always have what I need, wherever I'd go. Even though I was alone, I did not picture myself as lonely.

I know I used to have this fantasy, because it's in the Archive: I wrote about it on an undated piece of notebook paper (maybe 20 years ago? 30?).

I remember remembering this dream, even if I have no in-my-head memory of it any longer.

Looking back, I understand that my wagon could take me out of the hold-fast house, somewhere not far and I'd be in motion, feeling safe and free...

TRAVEL TALES

Scrawled notes from a visit back to California in 2003:

what being here allows me to see
(& smell)—
> *the sensuous—jacaranda*
> *princess tree*
> *mexican sage*
> *furry tongues extended*

wanting to feel   stripped to the skin
bathed in
> *flowers &   wind*

...as if California were the only place I could be sensuous: could feel things, from a light play of wind on my bare arms to an internal register of contentment, observing the glow of those purple flowers (what was their name?) at dusk—the daylight passing into flowery radiance.

Yet full summer in Louisville, when it was still relatively new, meant *full*: as in trees in full, heavy branch, drooping leaf, cicadas in full cry; clouds piling up, mounting over the flat and placid Ohio Valley; cumulus, to accumulate, buoyantly in the blue-charged heavens.

As if California were the only place—
but there is no "only" place...

<u>2008, Louisville</u> (scribbled on loose sheets of paper, from the Archive)

—I know I will be in Edinburgh three weeks from today. Somehow all the work will get done, I'll kiss my cat and leave her with the woman I'm paying to stay here in my space (sleep in my bed, poke among my books, look at my pictures). I'll arrive safely and splurge on a taxi from the airport, it will be a sunny morning and my insides will be craving 4 am sleep; and once the kind lady whose room I've rented has oriented me, I'll be off again, to totter in wonder through streets I fell in love with two years ago (remembering to look right when I cross, so I don't get run over). I don't know who will sit by me on the plane, I don't know who I will talk to in a café, I don't know if I'll even say a word to anyone until I board the mini-van for the Isle of Skye five days later. I don't know if I want to continue being a professor of English, I don't know if I want to stay in Louisville, I don't know if I can escape the spell of my ex-husband, I don't know if I can fall in love again, I don't know if my friends will even miss me; I'm entering menopause and the next "half" of life wavers like a heat-vision at the horizon and I don't want to be so alone, anymore.

All of this—about to be transported over the pond, because of the beautiful accident of Scotland...

In 2006, your ex-husband generously gifted you with enough frequent flyer miles to get to Edinburgh and back, and that's where you and Dorit (Israeli friend and roommate from long ago) got to experience the "Fringe Festival." It was your first time in the UK, first time in Scotland, first time in Edinburgh, and you could also speak Hebrew with Dorit and pretend the stone walls up the hill in Marchmont where you stayed jointly in a B&B were like the stone of Jerusalem (if not its walls). For eight days you both wandered through crowds, constant cheer, sunshine and warmth (an unusual welcome), music, balloons, bubbles, though you can barely remember the actual events you attended (a theater piece? a South African gospel choir...).

—At the B&B you and Dorit had your own little wing with small kitchen—and a dish soap called "Fairy." You discovered dark chocolate-covered ginger cookies and hot potato-and-pea hand pies. Evenings lasted forever, even in early August, and you do remember one night when the two of you took a "haunted" tour of the famous graveyard behind the famous church where "wee Bobby"—the terrier whose small statue is a tourist landmark—was said to roam at night (as well as any number of other ghosts, none of whom you detected, though the tour leader did manage a good fright at the very end).

Scotland meant: Edinburgh at the Fringe, which meant:
men in actual kilts; bagpipes; Old Town; 24-hour festivity; kind people with a lightly mocking sense of humor (especially for themselves); a poetry library; history, haunts and magic.

Of course you would go back.

*

In 2008 came Hawthornden, a writing program located at a small castle in Lothian, not far from a town called Bonnyrig and about 45 minutes on a bus to Edinburgh. —I'd applied for an "international writing fellowship" there. In the application, I wrote:

If accepted at Hawthornden for a Residential Fellowship, I will continue to map out and develop a manuscript of creative nonfiction for my book: "Forgetting Jerusalem." This book, incorporating both memoir and research, centers on the question of what "home" means to me as an American Jew and the granddaughter of Polish and Russian immigrants. In exploring this question, I am in part reacting to the nearly universal obsession among American Jews to inculcate in their children a Zionist-Jewish identity. Young people (ages 18 to 26) are routinely offered "birthright" trips to Israel at no or very low-cost, that consciously work to create an attachment to the "Jewish homeland." I myself have longstanding connections to Israel, beginning with a baccalaureate junior year abroad some thirty years ago. However, as an adult returnee to Yiddish—the language and culture of my grandparents—and as a long-time critic of Israeli government policies, I cannot accept the American Jewish status quo. I want my book, written in poetic, evocative, yet urgent language (and intended primarily though not exclusively for an American Jewish audience) to create an alternate pathway into the notion of Jewish "home."

I continued for two paragraphs, and ended by saying:

I spent one week in Edinburgh in August 2006 and fell in love with Scottish landscape and culture. Scotland definitely feels like it could be one of my own personal "homes"—and I think I'd find it very nourishing to pursue my project at your retreat...

My application was accepted for the month of September 2008, where I was one of six writers, spanning genres, from Ireland, Australia, Poland, Canada as well as the U.S.

Hawthornden was (is) situated on a bluff above the River North Esk, and my room, up a spiral staircase to the attic floor where most of us stayed, overlooked the river and the forest on its opposite bank. I spent a lot of time just peering out that window, attending to the hoo-hooing of owls and the river's brisk current.

When I applied to Hawthornden, there was little to no information about it online. Today there is more, but one still has to send a letter to the program Administrator requesting an application—which is returned via post, as well. There is still no wifi at the castle.

And a glance online has refreshed much that I did not remember about the place: for example, the fact that the castle, completed in 1638 by the Scottish poet William Drummond, was built around the ruins of a 15th-century tower. I forgot that there are caves carved out of the rock beneath Hawthornden, that had apparently been used for hiding and defense by Bronze Age Celts and, in the 14th century, the Scottish king, Robert the Bruce. Yes, it was a very old and layered place, though I was mostly entranced by the knotted, twisted trees on the path leading up to the castle, which seemed to still exist in a fairy tale.[19]

---

[19] I'd also forgot that the castle was owned (and the literary residency founded) by Drue Heinz, whose third marriage brought her into millions, which she generously gave to the support of literature and writers in the States and in the UK. In 2018 she passed away, in her living quarters at Hawthornden, and a headline in the Edinburgh News stated: "Heinz Beans Widow Dies in Lothian Castle."

The internet further informs that Hawthornden was visited in 1773 by Dr. Samuel Johnson and James Boswell (which did sound familiar), and on the 14th of September, 1842, by Queen Victoria and Prince Albert (not so much), and that the residency program's alumni include Alisdair Gray, Helen Vendler, Ian Rankin and others of literary prominence. —The latter I had banished from my mind. I'm not sure how my (much more modest) group wound up at the castle, but we were there as pampered guests.

My scattered memories revolve around the creature comforts: baskets filled with lunch hauled up to our third floor by the housekeeper, and a constant supply of home-baked shortbread and tea just a short walk away in the "linen room." The housekeeper regularly freshened our sheets and plumped the comforters on our beds, and did our personal laundry.

Our bathroom contained a gigantic tub under a skylight. —Sitting in that tub on a rainy afternoon is one of my best memories...

Our hall floor creaked, day and night.
We sometimes poked our heads out, laughing nervously (ghosts? in a centuries-old castle? You must be kidding...).

Before dinner, we had to report to "sherry hour" in the "garden room."
Evenings, we were served coffee and cookies or cake in a semi-formal "drawing room" with a working fireplace.

Perhaps I will actually write my proposed book one day; I did knock out the bare bones of several chapters. But my time at Hawthornden—bordered by my stay in Edinburgh and a three-day tour of the Highlands beforehand,[20] and by several days in London afterwards—was given over mostly to thinking about poetry, occasionally writing it and to keeping a fragmentary journal, from which the following excerpts drift out of the *digital* Archive: the shade of who I was, then—

More than the "shade": consider these fragments as evidence, prooftexts of a new phase of my life...

8/31/08

Rain since I got here, & having left the laptop in the coordinator's car, I couldn't really —
sink-in.
So, quickly assembling a temporary home—
my things out of suitcases, the modest box I shipped here—

Edinburgh, Anna Caro, an artist[21]—I felt sad to leave her & her family.
a fancied attachment

---

[20] The small tour company was called "Rabbie's"—after the eternal Scottish poet laureate, Robert Burns.

[21] The first time I'd stayed with her, having found her through a B&B booking agency. Whenever I'm back in town, I let her know so we can meet, have a proper catch-up. "Just give me a bell," she will say.

—the lilt of their speech, I begin to copy its patterns (consciously/unconsciously).

People I grab at:
"these—my people"—well, yes, I felt enormously comfortable there;
the sense of humor (Anna looked over the railing at the E-burgh festival Theatre, from "the gods,"[22] to wonder what would happen if something dropped from up there, and knocked over her glasses case)—
Brigitte, the German woman, with whom I sat last night (again "in the gods"), awaiting the dervishes[23] (who didn't come till the second half)—who presents her "story" in brief as a never-knowing for sure where her Home is, moving from Germany to Scotland and back (and Holland, in-between):
"Ever since I was a child, I wanted to go out into the world—<u>fern</u>" (the German word, meaning "distance"—close to the Yiddish <u>forn</u>, to travel)—& then, she'd be feeling <u>heimweh</u>, homesick (the Yiddish, again, so close, <u>heymvey</u>)—and back and forth. She "gets restless"; she's not sure she'll ever settle down.
A soulmate!...of sorts. —Collecting people, my people (and her face, another that could've come from a Renaissance painting, like those of so many people I saw on the flight from Amsterdam).

"But what is home, is it a place, or people, or where your roots are?" I asked her. "Well, I think it's got to be people," she said.... Though hastily adding, "If a place feels right, that counts too."

---

[22] That is, the highest balcony.

[23] I could never have imagined then that I would be part of a Sufi circle in Louisville, Kentucky, where a dervish would turn while we chanted.

Edinburgh—I felt at-home there, at moments; talking to a woman in line for ice-cream at the theater last night (a fancy theatre!...yet the ice cream, delivered as if at a ballpark)... The gorgeousness of the vistas on the Rabbies tour: the soft sounds of "gallic"[24]...just: dreaming, dreaming of—becoming an ex-pat, of living w/friendly artsy people who speak with lilting tongues...

Sept 1ˢᵗ—
day begins in splendor of sun, walking and gawking, taking pictures—

now (as the housekeeper predicted) the clouds clot up again, more rain is in the works— ground already so spongy it thickens into lapping mud, it weeps water.

a hush has fallen, broken only by the occasional crow.   or owl. writers in their rooms...

and I'm feeling still that I'm hovering...standing a little apart from myself, my work (is there a distinction?) I feel so far from American, Jewishness, and Israel here! and it's a pleasure... my home strapped to my back.

perhaps I should write about that.

---

[24] The word for Scottish Gaelic is written "Gaidhlig" and sounds like "gallic."

Sept 4th (I think)…I could easily lose track of days here.
so beautiful out this morning—clear!…I did the Castle Walk alone & heard, before I saw,
two small deer break out of thicket in bramble above & to the left…
a gift.

9/5/08

sitting on the stone steps outside the Garden Room at the castle, at the promontory
overlooking (overhearing) the river Esk—

—"Scotland" a beautiful border, a quirky unusual backdrop—
& I affiliate with it, in a strange (temporary) way-
so open, wide-ranging & filled with people & possibilities: against the shallow narrows of
the city in which I've made my (temporary) home.

At breakfast I talk about rejecting the US, becoming an ex-pat (the current fantasy)—young
T, who lives in Los Angeles, in a different America: "why don't you just leave Louisville?"

—to hoover rugs
—right, right-i-o
—no dog fouling
—surname
—biscuits
—fagged; shattered [those mean tired]

(a plethora of different terms & expressions, I'm not recollecting them right now)

Is <u>home</u>, [even a temporary one!] something you can just: leave?

*

I don't even know if I can go to the dark places or even
—the way my 20 y.o. self used to feel called-to by poems, or shut out from the place—
there was a Place inside I used to go—

Tues 9/[just had to check] 9

—another day of rain (after yesterday's temporary swathes of sun)—

the long precious unspooling bolt of time, here; sometimes—static, dreary—
sometimes...needing to shake it up.

last nite—watching <u>39 Steps</u> on Moy's computer, preceded by her sock puppet theatre.

today...
accepting (acknowledging that is): I will be back in Louisville;
needing to face facts there (the need to squirrel away money; ...to figure out—
my escape?!...).   toward people?   or place.

—Cathy here talks often of her life in New Brunswick & her husband;
Moy, so completely at ease w/herself, vivacious, a bubbling fount of words—& she too, about
her husband, a bit about her daughters;
Tiffany has her posse; Petra, her "partner"; Leshek appears to be married.
—& I—I am relatively silent;
in part, floating detached from things,
my heart feeling: it does not blaze for any one.
It holds no one 'in it'.

ah—this reminds me (w/a diminutive spreading of my heart-flow)—
that I meant/intended to 'act as if'—
to continue to say: "at this time next year I will be married"—
as if I had already met him

and if "married" is not the right word then—
"by this time next year, I will be in a committed
I will be with my
I will—

9/14 (Sunday)
weather restored to its usual overcast, more appropriate gloom—

strange elastic quality of time, here.

& walking down the drive from the road to the Castle
  —two miniature deer flushed from the high right side of the road
—bounding across like puffs of smoke & gone

9/25 (thurs)

I've stared out the window here—a lot.
just stared at thick, thick layerings of trees, deciduous, evergreen—lofty roiling branches.

And even when I was sitting staring out the window at the furious tangle of dank, damp trees—at the "Lady Walk" on the bank opposite—even when I saw butterflies spin lazily up to that window, or a single feather from an invisible bird float down…

it was passing, "it"—the experience, time itself.

We are chained to the future (with a fine, shining filament).

*

I also wrote: *I couldn't appreciate being there any more than I did*—which must be true, and yet I feel a pang looking at the online photos, reading about the lack of wifi and the policies of in-castle silence between breakfast and sherry hour…the stringencies, the intensity intended and my own frequent floating when I was there, unable to root myself deeply in the writing; inattentive to the place's history, keeping my aperture relatively narrow. Those six weeks I spent in the UK represented my first solo travel, and I had not yet found a way to expand my sense of connection beyond the margins of my own anxieties.

But the future that tugged so incessantly as I passed through Hawthornden contained multiple trips back to the UK. I could swing them because I was working, teaching, in fact, a "four-four" load, and because my university operated on a system of six week "sessions" instead of semesters, so I could double up on courses during some sessions to keep another session free from the classroom. And I soon found a Scottish Jewish poet who I wanted to research (fell for, really—though he had died in the mid-1990s).

> *I did fall in love with London, with other English places I got to visit, with the*
> *feeling of the places, with the <u>feeling</u> I*
> > *projected on the places, with my body moving*
> *through the other side of the looking glass*
> *(look right, not left; queue left, not right).*

2011: Post-travel notes from England

—Hot tap water runs from very hot to scalding. There are no warning signs, as there would be in the U.S.; instead, I think, people must believe that you can just figure out how not to burn yourself, for goodness' sake.

—People in small towns create charming ways to package and sell their traditional culture; tourists complete the circle by agreeing to buy cheap reproductions of what is on offer. ("On offer"—an English idiom.)

—One reason to visit old places and old things: villages, cottages, castles, footpaths, glass cases containing tiny-waisted dresses, rooms containing beds built for very short people—is to encounter the past in material form. Nothing can take the place of <u>actually walking</u> the footpath; smelling the sweet grassy scent of, for example, West Yorkshire's summer moors; being present in the dining room at the Parsonage in Haworth where three young women, the Brontë sisters, spent their nights writing books in longhand at the table, and strolling arm-in-arm before the hearth.

—At the V & A (Victoria & Albert Museum) in London, I ate a brownie and drank tea in "refreshment rooms" more beautiful than any room I had <u>ever</u> sat in before, in my entire life. Despite everything I know about Empire that makes me shudder (*is that even the beginning of an ethical sentence? No, it is not; however, I will continue*)— despite "all that"—just walking in the hallways of the V & A filled me with tranquility and happiness. Everywhere, beauty: and not even so much the statuary, stained glass, gold-encrusted Buddhas, weeping Marys and Scottish paintings: it was more to do with the secret proportions of the halls themselves; tall ceilings that did not overwhelm; archways, and just the amount of available light-filled space in a given area (or dimness, through which painted angels could be seen hovering).

Available light.

And the pleasure of walking, practicing my city walk, my big city walk, the London walk, the way the legs churn in an open pattern and cover miles in between stops for tea.

*

It's a fairy tale power, this ability you have to fall in love with a landscape, with a country (the *idea* of Scotland, its history, its languages); to fall in love with Scottish people— represented by the handful you've actually conversed with as you stayed in their homes, as well as the many you've brushed past in streets, on trains, or purchased soap from at an art fair.

How does it begin?

Maybe it's the window you gaze out of on a train headed North—out of Glasgow, away from the grimy urban plain into foothills and slowly opening valleys. You're headed into the Highlands, their cleared-off mountains still reverberating with the brutal history staged there.

Maybe it's the first time the mountains get close: the train skittering among them, bouncing and clanging, its dense spout of steam whistling overhead—and the fringe of water, delicate lace on the backs of bare rock, the continual drizzle and seep of it, the fluids that feed the briny earth. You're in an upland of dense green through which the barrens peak, and of *upwelling*, a surge of countless freshets and the paths they make down the hills, their special name in Gaelic lost with all the other names you've tried to make a part of you.

—Maybe it's your own ignorance, your mis-belonging, as you convert every trestle into a sense of communion.... Yet:

—it's something you hear: a lonely call, as you're sitting on this ScotRail train car with a paper cup of tea, riding backward, so you never quite leave behind anything you've seen.

Yes, you're a tourist and yet (stubbornly): hearing this call brings joy.

Much later, it's a song: "Northumbrian Lullaby."
Even these two words have a music that—points at something—but it's the music itself, moving in a haunting key from low to high and drifting down, again and again, in children's voices on a recording called "Pleasure,"[25] that summons a sense of—*recognition*.

Yet—*I don't think I'd ever heard this before.*

But you did hear it, somewhere, between Edinburgh and York, in a kingdom that once existed hundreds of years ago, in a winter of sheep
     and *bairns* and a *lang nicht* and wind kicking up, from low to high

---

[25] By Malcolm Dalgleish and the Oolites

and drifting down again, in notes that do not resolve but sound like breath,
    a candle that shudders but turns away its own death,
        suggesting a warmth that does not quite exist
in bedded-down darkness.

*

And then, there was Arthur: A. C. Jacobs, Scottish Jewish poet, who had died unseasonably, not quite 57, in Madrid in 1994. He was a perfect literary companion in that he preferred to keep himself to the margins, restlessly traveled, had no children…

It was your Sabbatical pleasure to visit his little archive at his sister's house in North London. You needed to learn more, for after all—who *was* this poet? this man? He had written so many poems never published during his lifetime…. And like your other companion, Rosa Nevadovska, he'd had only one book of his poems out, and then after his death, friends published his "collected," having gone through these very folders, manuscripts and papers.

And you returned one last time to his archive after it had been housed at the University of Leeds (and were scolded for thoughtlessly over-fingering onionskin pages, which before you had touched with ardor, and without gloves).

One summer you planned a trip to Tobermory, because that's where Powell and Pressburger filmed *I Know Where I'm Going*, and that was one of your favorite films.

Oh the ironic confidence of the title, not only for the young woman depicted in the film, but the woman more than twice her age who watched it.

A piece of writing just fell out of an old notebook I was sifting through. Not my handwriting—my therapist's. Recording both sides of what she heard me say about going to Scotland yet again, a week before that scheduled trip:

7-15-14

It's OK to go even if you don't know why you're going. It's OK to go and feel the travel feeling like I'm part of a bigger world. Seeing. Doing it brings a sense of belonging and connects me in many ways.

[she drew a box and put this inside]: *You do have a reason for going, to write about this poet who loved Scotland.*

You could be at the beginning a new creative cycle.

[she drew a line]
You're too old and too tired to do this kind of thing. You should be getting organized and fixing things for school, so you won't feel so tired. You're gonna be sorry and it'll be your fault. You could be using this time to figure out what you want to do and so you're going to wind up stuck here and it will be your fault.

Traveling alone so much leads to you continuing to be alone and that's your fault too.

—and other fables…

July 2014, Isle of Mull

An island country can sprout—islands.
On the bus heading up over hills and down into Tobermory, I got mixed up:
Was that the mainland out there, reflecting light? —And calling across the water
to Mull (calved long ago yet still connected, because *the mainland
is an island*—
I saw it from the sky—
and the seagulls in Edinburgh and Glasgow know it too).

There is no being cut off from a mainland. Boats move constantly back and forth on the
churn, borne on the animate waters. I sense we travel not due to gasoline and engines
but the waves' consent,
bearing us up.

Upon arrival, it's good to be lodged at the Harbor Guest House, in harbor, encircled—
though alone.

*

I was lying on one of the twin beds in my room just now ("single supplement"), battered down by incessant sound of heavy drops on the skylight—when suddenly it got quiet.

The Italian couple next door who expressed themselves with so much animation, in their shower, in their bed, have gone.

The rain has not ceased, but it's much finer, and (kneeling beside the window) I can see out to rising puffs and curls of mist—ascending from the valley clefts out there, the other side of the Bay.

The sky so large here and so mutable, pierced by occasional birds (one in a tree yards down the hill just fanned a sizable white tail).

A smaller bird directs itself toward this window—comes to rest in a tree (I never know the names of trees except for maple, pine, oak, willow).

Smells of cooking meat waft up from the kitchen below. The couple running this B&B are nice enough but only interested in making sure the rooms are cleaned and knowing what they should make me for breakfast. Their Scottish accents are so thick that (for the first time in my travels to this land) I have a hard time catching every word.

My mobile phone with its London area code does not work up here...

A surprising amount of time can be spent watching mist rise from a distant valley—and the slant of rain, picking up, out there.

I've come to Scotland this time because it's been a few years and I wanted to remember what I love about it, so I can better understand how Arthur felt. Perhaps this is fantasy. It is immensely beautiful up here, and I've had some nice moments with local folks, mostly people selling me a book (in Tobermory Books and Tackle) or a cup of coffee, moments when the insider/outsider sense wore away, engaged in a familiar transaction of buying/selling, with its ancient exchange associations that make it feel as if it exists outside specific cultures.

> *You also spent an hour on Skype talking to a friend back in Louisville. It's the necessity of feeling seen as who you are, not just a tourist briefly taking up space in a café. It made you feel more embodied.*

Anyway, I'm still on my own here. It feels thrilling and scary to say it, even though everything's gone so well, and I leave tomorrow for more travels—lots of moving through space ahead, on various helpful land, sea and sky vehicles.

Did Arthur fetishize aloneness? He wrote:
My favorite word is loneliness.
It seems to cry out beyond love's lands
To the night's dark wildness...[26]

---

[26] "For No Words," in the *Collected*; p. 175

In his poems he often seems to be alone—on the sidelines—observing, absorbing, feeling, thinking, watching—himself as well as the scenes and transactions around him.

But I think he was a lover; certainly a romantic (self-described, no less). Women (who seem various, not the same one), or parts of them, arise in a number of his poems... breasts, skin, hands, lips. I have the sense that he was a quietly attractive man but not the easiest to get along with—or perhaps he chose to be with women who offered dramatic counterpoint to his own soft ways.

I read the trope of wandering in his writing as a rejection of a single home, a single identity or structure; and in my own romanticism, see myself reflected there.

Did I fetishize aloneness?

On my own, everything on my own (except for staying, whenever I did, at Anna's in Edinburgh, or that time at Moy's in Derby, or at Arabella's one summer off the Caledonian Road back in London...
and at the spiritual center in the Scottish Borders, a ready community in which I moved like a leaf caught in a gentle pool, around, around, soaking up the warming attention that came my way).

Alone in—the present moment.
Surrounded by people, so—never alone.

—There were the ones I stood in line with at 7 a.m. after my first transatlantic flight and no sleep, shifting forward in micro-movements toward passport control—under a stupefying ceiling light.

Pushing my too-heavy suitcase (and I *really* had not slept at all). Wanting to collapse, curl up on the floor; but we were all together, in tiny fractions of breath and forward movement.

And the man who stamped my passport.

And just the tide of people, as I caught a surge of wakeful energy, shouldering around me on the way to the Tube, speaking some of the 70 languages into which Moses had translated the Torah, their hair black or turbaned or curled against their scalps or plain Jane brown, accenting facial planes,

Britishers, Londoners, plus arrivals from everywhere, shouldering together in a rush toward the train, joined in anonymity, even if fixed anew in gravity and feet scraping the ground
—still in *flight*.

And on escalators up, up into Camden Market from the Tube, and in every Tube station I moved through, so many people, caught up in the flood, a part of the anonymous whole.

And on the streets, or watching from a café window where I ate wild mushrooms on toast—gently beating back the nerves I felt, keeping a skin of excitement and interest intact over the deep places where uncertainty pulsed.

Alone:
A bit of moving flesh, a spark, bouncing through international terminals, crossing through (albeit perfectly familiar and English-speaking) zones,
by myself.

And yet I felt more connected, there, to crowds of strangers than I often did in the home I had made in Louisville.

2017, Scotland again

Three years after Mull, you're back to the Western Isles, this time riding ScotRail all the way to Mallaig, where the ferry awaits to take you to the Isle of Skye for a short conversation course at the Gaelic College (where within a few days, you will have decided that your teacher, a native of the rougher sort, is a witch with her white hair and blue eyes, who has cursed you with her own legacy of insecurity and pain.)

But never mind.

That summer, with its constant going: over the Atlantic going into London where you were going on the Tube into Camden or Islington, going by train to Portsmouth to give a paper and going up to Glasgow from which you were going up to Mallaig and "over the sea to Skye" (just a channel really, a strait) and going to the Gaelic College, where so many dreams go, even now, like gilded moths.

Moments flare up:

—A meeting with an American woman at The Project Café in Glasgow, she'd been living there for a year studying Gaelic, it had been a rainy blustery day and she was almost manically pleased to meet with me—so much energy and positive power—she had done the hard thing, removed herself from the familiar for a full year, come on her own, shared a flat—for some reason I am seeing naked lightbulbs hanging from tall, chipped ceilings—it was exciting, my note-taking could barely keep up with her discoveries...

—And at the Gaelic college, asking for a cup of tea at the café (too scared to make a mistake in my skeletal conversational Gaelic, I rely on English even for this small thing), but looking out the windows at the landscape, I think *There's a one-year program I could do here, I could do it*, be here when the snow is blown horizontal across those hills, take refuge in the library, it wouldn't matter if I didn't really know anyone, we'd all be beginners together (and the books would, as usual, become companions).

—One foot in these imaginings, one on the real turf of my life in Louisville, professional job, my students, my Field Avenue apartment, my cat...

All the going, even in Edinburgh, from one rented room in Marchmont to another down in Leith, and your legs a blur of walking through the city, the Meadows, Peter's Yard Café, the waters of Leith, the going in-between.

When you're in Edinburgh in 2017, a series of coincidences make you feel like the stone-gray city has opened its pearly treasure just for you: you run into a woman from the language program, twice—a smart and snappy woman who happens to be 90, dressed in a pale pink coat, bobbing in the sidewalk flood of earnest walkers.

On another windy, rainy day, a fellow student from Skye invites you to come have lunch and talk with her and a Scottish storyteller in his spacious pre-Georgian flat. He's handsome, tall, with a full head of white hair and a raspy voice, betraying his age. And he wears a kilt and has made a pot of lentil soup and blesses everyone at table before they partake. And there's a gas fireplace lit and cups of Earl Grey and while he talks you're writing in your notebook, trying to catch every flower and jewel that falls from his mouth.

And then there is the couple who have moved from the spiritual center in the Borders where you once met them to a flat in Marchmont, and they too feed you lunch and patiently listen to your questions and make gentle suggestions for how you can follow your inclinations toward God, despite your way of moving in the world, which is to move and not be still; which is to search for, and not find.

And then there is the woman writer you've met who is also a Yiddish maven, who accompanies you on the train to Stirling for a special gathering of Yiddish students who welcome you at the home of their teacher, a strikingly tall, faintly red-headed woman of northern Irish extraction who is an accomplished Yiddish translator.

What does it mean to be so welcomed by a place? that you yourself are in love with?

—Perhaps it means your love applies much less to specific people and more to:
a landscape, and some ideas that have stuck in your head such as the fantasy of learning Gaelic (so you can communicate with the fairies, of course); and particular poems, particular figures of poets whose lives were often cripplingly difficult but whose verse lifts you through a parted veil.

It has meant:
so many visits, walking the same routes, visiting the same cafés and bookstores, the Poetry Library in Edinburgh and its Storytelling Center, visiting the same people, with whom you have no deep connection: just that of the traveler who comes to hear news of their lives. (And to share yours.) Blessing the same views from up on the Royal Mile, through this narrow stony aperture or that, or just out to the distant water or its twin, the swirling sky.

And *this* time, the tumblers have moved in such a way that the city seems to open up (a bit), embrace (take you in).

—But you were still only passing through: one of the wanderers, the ones who fill a space and then leave it empty for the next visitor.

"—OR ELSE IT'S ALL HOME"

So what's it like to stop?
The *goingness*.

Back in Louisville, in summer 2018: to the duplex on Field Avenue, a narrow street lined with spacious houses that cradles morning birdsong.

The *going* collects into the files and papers and books purchased in Edinburgh at Blackwell's but still unread. It is good to stop going, at least for a while, but of course there are tears because you love Scotland, and Edinburgh is one of your homes...

Last night you walked a couple miles in your own neighborhood and the warm dusk with its cool core that felt so familiar, extended past 9 p.m. —And then you thought of the walk you took on the campus last summer on Skye, where at 10 p.m. an eerie spectral lavender hovered across mainland mountains, a high breeze pushing pale streaks across the heavens, still filled with light: pink-powdered, gold-powdered light.

And tumbling into your student cot an hour later with the blinds drawn to create a sleepy darkness.

But still thrumming, vibrating out there, the restless incandescence.

*

In the summer of 2019, your move to Bloomington initiates more perspectives.

It's like this:
(with another twist of the lens, to stand back, apart from yourself, as you look):

M's plan is to move in with her boyfriend, from her place in this city to his house in a sweet, summer-quiet town in an adjacent state. This seems like the accustomed trajectory, from apartment to house, from singleness to duo, from self-obsession to mutual sharing.... She never thought such intimacy with one other, with a man, would occur again.

This means, of course, in addition to leaving her university teaching job (for which she is more than ready), leaving her apartment on Field Avenue. Since 2011 "home" has been this ground floor flat with battered pine beneath a few rugs, dulling paint job, cracks appearing in ceiling plaster and walls here and there. —Eight years: this span of time is actually the longest she has spent in any one dwelling since leaving Ramsey Place.

From here she has traveled solo, time and again, exploring while carrying this sense of home inside her. It's been her refuge after a week of teaching, a space in which to lurk, regarding angles of morning light in her writing room while standing in the hall, reading a few pages of an Ali Smith novel in the kitchen, then revolving into the bedroom and picking up a book by Barbara Pym. It's where she lets her gaze drift over the untouched volumes of Yiddish poetry that await her decision to open them, try to read them, maybe start to translate some bits of them.

Her things are positioned in ways that please her and the look of it pleases her and its relative smallness pleases her (like the smallness of the recently purchased used car, which she seems to wear as much as drive).

It's important for her to look and *see* things—especially her own things, the stuff collected in years of living alone that can speak back to her through the volume of silence and empty space that surrounds her and those things as well.
—It's the flyer from a coffee festival in London, a small brown paper bag stamped "Tobermory Books and Tackle," and the books that fill a dozen or more bookcase shelves, so important, even if she has not read them yet.

It's not that she is afraid (any longer, anyway) of emptiness, or rejects it: it surrounds her, after all, in ways that sometimes feel like an embrace. She just needs to be in communication, even when she is alone and silent. It is like a form of dolphin echolocation: it helps her locate herself.

So how can she desert her bedroom dresser with its mysterious mini-drawers that sit on its top, or the round table made of oak (or fake oak, she wasn't sure) at which she has hosted numerous tea parties with girlfriends, or the roll-top desk at which she stands right now, which looks antique but was really made in China, that she had bought for next to nothing at a local consignment store?

It's almost embarrassing; it feels like a confession of some major flaw to tell her boyfriend that what she most likes to do (besides take long walks when it's not hot outside, have tea and talk with girlfriends, and watch old movies) is to: read; write; ramble in libraries; peruse bookstores; and talk about writing with friends.

Is it possible she loves books more than people?

Books feel more like family than her remaining blood relatives (well, except for her brother). She used to go into her room as a teenage girl, shut the door on the rest of the house and lose herself in reading. She would lie on her stomach on the bed or on the floor, elbows easily propping her up, and just—read, dwelling inside another world.

In other words, she has lived more in virtual reality than in the "real" one, as much as possible.

Books, on the one hand; and on the other, the importance assigned to looking, seeing things to which personal history or past travel clings. There *must* be a reflection; she is otherwise invisible and has been all these years (fooling everyone along the way).

This man who tends his gardens, who bicycles for miles, who runs to raise funds for various causes, this man who cooks and tends to her…does he *see* her?

She does not see any reflection in him of her own life.

You are so unmaterialistic, her man friend tells her.
It's one of the things he admires.

It's true she does not crave more and more and more possessions, but—
words, books, language, travel—
she is, herself, possessed.

—What happened to this life of hers, when she moved into his?
—She consigned it to this book...

A Parting Glass

Indiana, a place of in-between. A land of counterpane? —No, despite farm-squares stitched together into homogeneous greens, browns, when seen from the sky. Fly-over country—yet nowhere to fly…because now it is "home."

My partner and I live together entwined, yet in parallel (and maybe that's how it's supposed to be, but I've never really known this before): evenings and mornings together (nights, too) and then long afternoons on our own.

Terry repairs to the woods as often as he can. He used to live in a house bordering state forest, long years with his late wife, raising their daughter (and goats and crops and grapes for making wine). I know it fulfills him, to walk at an urgent pace through familiar paths or bushwhack on "adventure walks" deeper into forests both known to him and still filled with mystery places, urging him on. And he's constantly bringing things into the material world surrounding our Bloomington house: chopping, sawing, hammering—or tilling, planting, gathering. New gates for the fence, a screened-in back porch, a chicken coop! And lavishly abundant vegetables and flowers.

And my "material" is words; often no one sees them but me.

I get entangled with my own thoughts, they grow like Sleeping Beauty vines and I become the prince who gets lost in them…

There are spaces that are mine within this shared house. Having moved here with 70 boxes of books, I swore never to buy any more—but after a while, that promise fell to the intense pleasure and lure of the new...I brush my hands across their spines, although I do not look at them with the same need for remembrance or reflection.

—But is this *home*?

It may not be: because acknowledging a single place as "home" feels like a betrayal of every other place that has felt like home.
—Just another feature of this way of being, of rootlessness by choice, the odd privilege of never owning a house nor bearing a child (weightiest of anchors).

Homes are variable, temperamental, flexible, bulging and shrinking with assigned meanings, finally disappearing into the pages of a notebook, where years ago a poet has written:

in the little house where I live

in the little house of sticks and feathers   in the little house of tarp and wind
moth-eaten cloth   and gold leaf

a sudden gust unlocks a door

something local like the sky
announces
its presence

                                        how far does a beam of
light go toward the stars?   —until it tires?

no,   it goes as far
      as a star can see

Not Done Yet

Writing is without boundaries
—in a world where people crossing boundaries may be detained, imprisoned, or repelled,
"sent back"—to a place that has its own boundaries that defy departure.

This is still happening in the world outside this book,
this book that wants to draw its own "final" boundary.

But how does a book confront its own restlessness, decide to "settle"—?

I find an unexpected articulation of my ways of being in excerpts from the blog of an herbalist, a naturalist (who, oddly enough, spends much of her time living in a borough of New York City):[27]

Judith Berger writes in May 2020 about a spot in New York's Catskill Mountains:

> *Yesterday I was at one of my favorite places of all time, where I have camped often, lying awake at night listening to nocturnal whisperings, watching stars…while I lie snug in my sleeping bag. It's one of those places I return to year after year, always in early May, and so it satisfies my internal requirement for pilgrimage. I hope I have*

---

[27] The herbalist and writer Judith Berger is an explorer of wild places and plants, a wild-crafter, and a Jew who grew up in Brooklyn. See www.judithbergerherbalist.com for more.

earned a kind of intimacy with the place, having gone out to meet it, often once or twice each year for 15 years....

I translate her words into my own experience:

[O]ne of my favorite places of all time, where I have flown to often, lying awake at night on the plane listening to nocturnal whisperings, watching stars...:
—is London.
— is Edinburgh.
These have been the places I return to year after year...and so they have satisfied my internal requirement for pilgrimage. I hope I have earned a kind of intimacy with these places, having gone out to meet them, often once or twice each year for 15 years....

Although Berger's "pilgrimages" are into the wilds, what she says resonates and I thank her for giving me these words.

But then she turns to John Muir, that foundational naturalist, saying:

> *...in returning to these gathering places over and over I have, in some way, encountered the felt-sense experience that Muir wrote of:—that the Earth, in particular, the Catskill mountains, is in me. The internalization of this lovely otherness/kindredness to which I am repeatedly called, fills something in myself, and gives my nervous system and heart greater stability in difficult times, and at times, returns to me the ground under my feet.*

What this refers to seems so primal I have to ask myself:
Is the Earth—in *me*?
I have rarely felt *"the ground under my feet"* in this metaphorical or even literal way.

Not for long, anyway.

What is *"in me"* that *"gives my nervous system and heart…stability in difficult times"*—?

Words. Language. And—the "forests of gestures manifest in [city] streets."[28]

---

[28] From "Walking in the City," a chapter in Michel de Certeau's book *The Practice of Everyday Life.*

City:

built, artifactual;
a place of sharing that is impersonal yet embodied, a tight embrace with room
for each one,
where to walk means passing through openings in between
other peoples' bodies, and your body sometimes brushes
others if the streets are thick and

people move at a tempo unfamiliar yet
charged & you wish to keep up with it while adjusting to
a new angle of light & the way it reflects off walls
of adjacent buildings, office windows, sanctuaries, literary monuments

—the delight of sharing with other humans, anonymously, that
"lovely otherness/kindredness" that Judith Berger mentions.

Or (the Archivist notes) as I wrote in a poem in the winter of 1978:

Dream

just the lovely sense of
running through the streets at
night, from place to place as if
this city, the world
were my house & all the people,
my family
Roaming through my
house like a child at night
Night
dissolving boundaries   we are all
the same

About the Author

Merle Lyn Bachman is the granddaughter of a numbers runner, an opera buff, a tailor forced to raise chickens and a woman whose heart was so big, it failed too soon: in other words, ordinary Jews who immigrated to the U.S. (New York) from Russia and Poland in the early 20th century.

During some of her own migrations, she has published the following poetry chapbooks and books: *The Opposite of Vanishing* (EtherDome), *Wrecker's Ball* (Finishing Line), *Diorama with Fleeing Figures* (Shearsman), *Blood Party* (Shearsman) along with *Nameless Country*, an anthology of poetry by A. C. Jacobs, co-edited with Anthony Rudolf (Carcanet), and *Recovering Yiddishland* (Syracuse University), a book of literary criticism and translation. In 2015-16 she was a Translation Fellow of the Yiddish Book Center and is currently developing a manuscript of selected poems by Rosa Nevadovska, in translation.

Lightning Source UK Ltd.
Milton Keynes UK
UKHW030904160522
403067UK00007B/616